P
for ROSH

The Rosh Hodesh Table
Foods At The New Moon

Jewish Women's Monthly Festivals

By
Judith Y. Solomon

BP

Biblio Press   *New York*

DEDICATION

For my mother, who always puts food on my plate.
For the women throughout Jewish history who celebrated Rosh Hodesh.

Library of Congress Catalog Card Number 95-77510
The Rosh Hodesh Table: Foods At The New Moon
Jewish Women's Monthly Festivals
by Judith Y. Solomon
ISBN 0-930395-23-9

Cover by Mark Lerer and Juan Tenorio
Type/Design by Rivanne Advertising

Printed in the United States of America

ACKNOWLEDGMENTS

I would like to thank these special people:

My parents, my friends, and Michael, my wonderful husband, whose support and advice were irreplaceable. The Reference Frame Writers Workshop (Tom, Michael, Lucy, Ann, Hardy, and Paul), for their critiques and encouragement. Mordechai Housman of Pearls of Myrrh Judaic Research Center, Judaica consultant and good friend, for critiquing and technical advice; Chava Boylan, for her research suggestions. Rabbi Yehoshua Leiman, who took the time to discuss Shaloch-Manot and the Omer over the phone. Rabbi Shmuel Teich and Zechariah Honikman, for their phone consultations on Tu B'Shevat. Christine St-Jean, who found source material on the history of kashrut. Arlene Agus, Rivka Haut, Blu Greenberg, Sally Rappeport, and Linda Safron, who talked to me about Rosh Hodesh. Thanks to the very knowledgeable librarians at Stern College and the New York Public Library Jewish Division; and of course, Eliyahu Ki Tov- for writing <u>The Book of Our Heritage</u>! If errors are found, they shall be corrected in any later printing.

And last but not least, a special thank you to Doris B. Gold, my editor and publisher, without whom this book could not be.

ABOUT THE AUTHOR

Judith Y. Solomon has completed many years of religious education in Yeshiva day schools, including one year in Israel at Midrashet Moriah. She is a graduate of Stern College for Women of Yeshiva University, NY, with a degree in English Communication and an Associate of Arts in Judaic Studies.

She is a freelance public relations writer and manuscript reader, and also co-leads Reference Frame, a NYC genre science fiction/fantasy/horror workshop. This is her first book.

"Our Sages said:
All your deeds should be for the sake of heaven,
even things of choice,
such as eating, and drinking…"

(Shulchan Aruch Orach Chayim, Hilchot Berachot 231:1)

"The Table is like an altar,
and the meal an offering."*

*(Rabbi Moshe Iserlis,
on the Shulchan Aruch Orach Chayim,
Hilchot Bitziyat Hapat, 167:5)*

*See Elul chapter.

A Rhyme For Moon Months

TISHREI starts with Rosh Hashanah,
CHESHVAN follows after;
KISLEV brings us Chanukah
With dreidels, games and laughter.
First comes TEVET, then SHEVAT—
A time when trees are planted;
ADAR retells the Purim plot,
At NISAN plagues are chanted.
In IYAR, there is Lag B'Omer,
SIVAN'S Torah-tended,
TAMMUZ, AV, ELUL, are next,
And the Jewish year is ended!

*By Dorothy Ross & Doris B. Gold; with permission from THE YOUNG JUDEAN MAGAZINE.

THE ROSH HODESH TABLE:
FOODS AT THE NEW MOON

By Judith Y. Solomon

Table of Contents

A Short Note On The Jewish Calendar

The Jewish year starts with <u>Tishrei</u>, at the beginning of Autumn. It is a time of internal reflection and transformation, and it begins with Rosh Hashanah, one of the holiest days of the Jewish year. Yet <u>Tishrei</u> has competition from <u>Nisan</u>, the month in which we began our Exodus from Egypt. Religiously and nationally, the Exodus is so significant that the Torah commands us to consider <u>Nisan</u> the first month of the year, <u>Iyar</u> the second, etc., leaving us with two different sequences for the months. In each chapter, I have recorded the number of the month by both systems.

May you have a bright and fruitful year!

Judith Y. Solomon

This etching of 1726 shows the New Moon being blessed in the courtyard of a Furth, Germany synagogue. (This custom is still observed the world over)

THE ROSH HODESH TABLE

Preface

The Jewish preoccupation with food is legendary. The Torah is filled with images of food. Israel is the land of milk and honey. Samson tore a lion in two and found honey in its stomach. It's amazing how many Jewish cookbooks appear each year. Go into any store and browse the cookbook section. There are books with recipes, with food history, with food metaphors... you name it!

Jewish women did not buck tradition here. The Torah describes the Matriarchs using food to good purpose. Sarah, Abraham's wife, fed the visiting angels cakes, milk, and later, meat. Rebecca prepared two kid goats in her plot to win Jacob his father's blessing. Their descendants are still busy with food. From Hadassah and B'nai Brith meetings to National Council events, Jewish women are as involved with food in their workplace as they are in their homes.

Eating is also an integral part of the Jewish calendar. All our festivals have some food link: Purim is the time of the hamantash, Rosh Hashanah the holiday of honey... Each holiday and season has an individual flavor because of its special food customs.

We may satisfy our sweet tooth at Rosh Hashanah, but the taste of apple and honey becomes more meaningful when we savor the symbolism behind it. Knowing the spiritual roots of our food customs adds an additional spice to the smorgasbord of the Jewish calendar.

But there are already more than enough books which discuss the Jewish holidays. The Rosh Hodesh Table focuses instead on the traditional aspects of Rosh Hodesh, the celebration of the New Moon, a holiday which binds all the festivals together. Even though Rosh Hodesh has become a minor festival, it was equated in the prophets with Shabbat, and with the big three (Passover, Shavuot (the Festival of Weeks) and Succot (The Festival of Booths)).[1] In ancient times, Rosh Hodesh determined when our holidays were observed. We would scan the heavens for the New Moon, and people from all parts of Israel would head for Jerusalem to testify that they had seen it. Then the Sanhedrin (High Court) would declare that it was Rosh Hodesh, thus determining when our holidays were celebrated. This Kiddush Hachodesh, or Sanctification of the Month, disappeared in 359 C.E with the establishment of a set calendar.[2]

Rosh Hodesh is the most frequent festival of the Jewish year. Passover, Purim and Chanukah appear only once. Like dear friends who have come for a visit, we enjoy their company and the happiness they bring. When they leave, we must wait a full year for their return. In contrast, Rosh Hodesh is a faithful visitor. She stops by not once, but eleven times![3] With the exception of Tishrei,[4] Rosh Hodesh is celebrated once a month at the first appearance of the New Moon.

The holiday has yet another distinction: it is a special holiday for women. According to tradition, women were rewarded with a greater part in Rosh Hodesh for two good deeds. First, they refused to participate in the sin of the Golden Calf. The women would not contribute their gold jewelry to create the idol; their husbands brought their own gold. Second, these women were among the first to contribute to the building of the Tabernacle.[5] For these two acts, Rosh Hodesh became a special woman's holiday.[6] Although all Jews observe this day, women have traditionally abstained from work. According to Rashi, women would not sew, spin, or weave on Rosh Hodesh,[7] the skills which they brought to the building of the Tabernacle. The Jerusalem Talmud validates this custom in Tractate Ta'anit, 1:6. There is much discussion in later sources about what kinds of work women could or could not do.[8]

Some people celebrate with a Rosh Hodesh feast,[9] or by learning the laws of Rosh Hodesh.

Why give women Rosh Hodesh and not some other holiday? The three major holidays mentioned were already assigned to our forefathers; but beyond that, Rosh Hodesh was the logical choice because of the traditional connections between women and the moon. Like a woman, the moon has its own cycle. Every month, after a short "hidden" phase when it is not seen at all, the moon is born as a tiny sliver in the sky. That small crescent, called the New Moon, grows steadily until it reaches its peak, a full sphere lighting up the night sky. Then the moon begins its decline, waning in size and stature until it disappears completely. But its light is renewed again a few days later when the New Moon reappears.

The woman's cycle is also one of birth, death, and rebirth. At the beginning of her menstrual cycle, a tiny egg, a potential life, grows in her. If nothing happens to bring it to fruition, it is lost, and the woman is left bereft. But the next month a new egg appears, and the woman is renewed seven days into her cycle with immersion in the mikveh (ritual bath)[10].

In Midrashic and Talmudic sources, the moon symbolizes femininity. The Talmud mentions that the moon and the sun were originally the same size, and that the moon was made smaller as a punishment for its arrogance.[11] However, the moon is destined to regain her stature, without becoming identical to the sun.[12] Similarly, women have been promised a renewal in the world to come.[13]

Despite these symbolisms, Rosh Hodesh began to be seen as a free day rather than a holy day in some circles. By the seventeenth century, women had apparently begun to do laundry during their free time, and by the twentieth century, the practice of abstaining from work on this holiday was far less prevalent. Then, in 1972, a group of women rediscovered the female connection to Rosh Hodesh and began observing the day with a special ceremony and feast. An article written by Arlene Agus, one of the members of the group, brought Rosh Hodesh to the attention of the feminist community.[14] Soon these "Rosh Hodesh Groups," societies of women who would gather to observe Rosh Hodesh, were popping up throughout the Orthodox, Conservative, and Reform communities. Like the moon, these groups would wax and wane; when one group stopped meeting, another might form in a neighboring community.[15] Their activities varied, from learning and discussion sessions to actual prayers and rituals.

Why did the Rosh Hodesh movement grow? The women involved speak of a renewed feeling of connection to our tradition. Sally Rappeport, the organizer of a now inactive Rosh Hodesh Group in Brooklyn, spoke of "women creating a different kind of space, a place to celebrate being Jewish with other women."[16] Linda Safron, whose group ended their meetings in November 1993, said that members often found it easier to learn about their tradition in the informal atmosphere of the Rosh Hodesh Group.[17]

However, contrary to some impressions, traditional Rosh Hodesh rituals do not exclude women. There are three such rituals currently practiced: the Rosh Hodesh blessing, the addition of special prayers on Rosh Hodesh day, and Kiddush Levana, the sanctification of the moon. The additional prayers can be said with or without a minyan (quorum of ten men), so women can say them at home or in their synagogue. The Rosh Hodesh blessing is recited on the Shabbat before Rosh Hodesh, between the Shemonah Esrai and Musaf prayers. It should be said in a minyan, but women and men may recite it on their own.

Kiddush Levana is more controversial. Some say that women can not say it at all, because according to Lurianic Tradition, the moon was made smaller as a punishment for Eve's sin. The feminine symbol was diminished, even as Eve herself was punished. Therefore, it would not be fitting for women to sanctify the moon.

What is Kiddush Levana? It's an almost mystical experience, that can happen on any night from 72 hours after the Molad[18] until approximately 14 days, 18 hours, and 22 minutes into the lunar cycle.[19] Most people do it on the Shabbat night after Rosh Hodesh. We gather in a minyan,[20] under the open sky when the moon is clearly visible, and recite a special prayer. The prayer is a celebration of the majesty of God's creations. We begin by reciting Psalms 148, "Hallelujah! Proclaim the praise of God from the heavens, proclaim it from the high places..." Amidst praise for God's celestial glory and protection, we speak of an orderly universe. He keeps His promise to renew the moon, the glorious crown of mankind, each month, and we praise Him for His wonders.

Do not confuse the Sanctification of the Moon with the Sanctification of the Month, which was the Sanhedrin's declaration of Rosh Hodesh. The latter has to do with the calendar; the former symbolizes our recognition of God's kindness in providing us with an organized natural system.[21]

Now that we have discussed the Jewish tradition of food and the feminine tradition of Rosh Hodesh, the obvious question is why connect Rosh Hodesh and food? After all, the title of this book is not <u>Rosh Hodesh</u>. It's <u>The Rosh Hodesh Table</u>: <u>Foods</u> at the <u>New Moon</u>.

All of the Rosh Hodesh leaders whom I consulted agreed that though they never consciously focused on food, refreshments became a central part of their meetings. According to Linda Safron, food became part of the sharing experience of her group. "One time I walked into someone's kitchen," she said. "We were preparing food together, talking as we were doing it... Once we ate, after the formal part of the program, we would talk." And Linda noted that one particular woman always brought olives, which became her symbol for the group.[22]

As a modern woman, it's hard to get excited about Rosh Hodesh. Twelve months pass, marked by holidays and seasons, and often one month seems like the next, filled with cooking, children and work; from Passover to Rosh Hashanah, the days fly like papers blowing on a New York street corner.

But everyone relates to food. You can smell it, taste it, and roll it around on your tongue. And as mentioned, holiday foods have their own symbolism and history, which adds that extra texture of spirituality.

Therefore, with pride I present a book which combines these two very old traditions: the celebration of the New Moon, and the food which has for centuries been a major part of the Jewish experience. The text is, of course, based on the beliefs and practices of traditional women, although it is known that women who are unaffiliated have been drawn to this monthly observance out of curiosity and wonder.

The book is divided into thirteen sections, one for each lunar month (including the leap month, Adar Beit.) Each section describes one or two (or more) different foods and their links to that month. If you love to cook, or even if you love to eat, you'll enjoy reading the fun food facts contained in this volume. Recipes are included so that you can experiment and enjoy the fruits of your knowledge.

Bon Appetit- and Ta'am Tov (Good Taste)!

Judith Y. Solomon
May, 1995

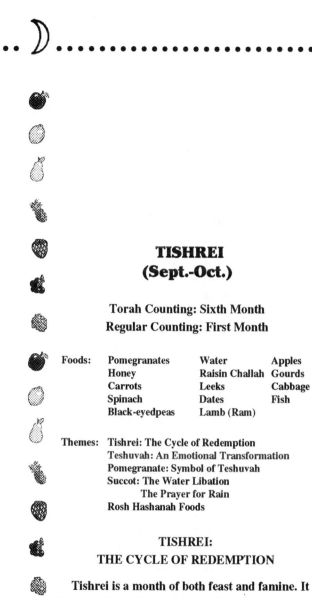

TISHREI
(Sept.-Oct.)

Torah Counting: Sixth Month
Regular Counting: First Month

Foods:			
	Pomegranates	Water	Apples
	Honey	Raisin Challah	Gourds
	Carrots	Leeks	Cabbage
	Spinach	Dates	Fish
	Black-eyedpeas	Lamb (Ram)	

Themes: Tishrei: The Cycle of Redemption
Teshuvah: An Emotional Transformation
Pomegranate: Symbol of Teshuvah
Succot: The Water Libation
The Prayer for Rain
Rosh Hashanah Foods

TISHREI:
THE CYCLE OF REDEMPTION

Tishrei is a month of both feast and famine. It begins at Rosh Hashanah, the Jewish New Year, with two days of apples and honey, of kiddush and celebration. The Torah commands us to feast and be merry on Rosh Hashanah, even though it is the Day of Judgment. Each person is judged by God and must account and repent for the past year's sins- a time which should call for solemnity and introspection. Instead, we are told to rejoice.

We were quite sad when we returned to the land of Israel after the Babylonian exile; on that Rosh Hashanah, we realized we had sinned and cried bitterly. Ezra the Scribe, our spiritual leader, commanded us to stop, saying, "Go, eat choice foods and drink sweet wines. . . <u>do not be sad</u>, for rejoicing in the Lord is the source of your strength."[3]

The Rabbis were puzzled by Ezra's words. They wondered: why should we be joyous on such a solemn day? They compared the Jew on Rosh Hashanah to one awaiting a judge's verdict. But God is not a local court judge; He is merciful and beyond human corruption. Those who approach Him on Rosh Hashanah pray with the confidence that God will, in His love and mercy, judge us favorably[4]. So Ezra told our people that all of their sins should not stop their celebration. Eat, drink, and be festive!

But food gives way to fast. Ten days later, on Yom Kippur, all thoughts of food vanish. The Day of Atonement is a solemn time, when we should not eat, drink, wear leather shoes, wear perfume, wash (although one may wash up to the knuckles for cleanliness and purity), or engage in sexual relations.[6] The seriousness of Yom Kippur is far removed from the happiness of the Jewish New Year.

In another five days, the pendulum swings back again. Succot, called *z'man simchateinu*,

JUDGMENT DAY

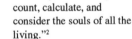

Rosh Hashanah is not called *Yom Hadin* or Judgment Day in the Torah. This is an oral tradition mentioned in the Mishnah, Talmud, and prayers.[1]

The prayer "Unitanah Tokef (Let Us Now Relate the Power)" describes God as a tender and merciful judge: "Like a shepherd pasturing his flock, making sheep pass under his staff, so shall you cause to pass, count, calculate, and consider the souls of all the living."[2]

DAY OF AFFLICTION

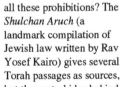
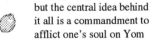

Ever wonder <u>why</u> we have all these prohibitions? The *Shulchan Aruch* (a landmark compilation of Jewish law written by Rav Yosef Kairo) gives several Torah passages as sources, but the central idea behind it all is a commandment to afflict one's soul on Yom Kippur.[5]

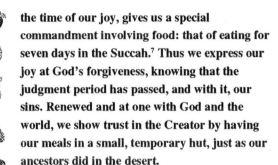

SUCCAH: THE FIRST MITZVAH

Rabbi Chaim Nussbaum says that on Sukkot, we show Teshuvah Me'ahavah, repentance out of love of God and His commandments. We return to God cleansed of our sins, determined to do His mitzvot. And the first one we do is sit in the succah![8]

WHAT IS TESHUVAH?

Rabbi Joseph Dov Soloveitchik, in his book *On Repentance,* describes it as a slow, inner metamorphosis which can take either minutes or years. It begins with an overall feeling of regret, an awareness of loneliness and of moral bankruptcy. Teshuvah is usually not tied to one specific deed; it grows until it brings one to an inner metamorphosis. By the end of repentance, we are ready to acknowledge sin (otherwise known as *viduy*).[9]

NEITHER RIGHTEOUS NOR WICKED

On Rosh Hashanah, God opens up three books: the book of the righteous, the book of the wicked, and the book of those who are neither righteous nor wicked. While He signs and seals the first two books on Rosh Hashanah,

the time of our joy, gives us a special commandment involving food: that of eating for seven days in the Succah.[7] Thus we express our joy at God's forgiveness, knowing that the judgment period has passed, and with it, our sins. Renewed and at one with God and the world, we show trust in the Creator by having our meals in a small, temporary hut, just as our ancestors did in the desert.

TESHUVAH:
AN EMOTIONAL TRANSFORMATION

The emotional cycle of Tishrei, from joy to solemnity and back to joy, is a reflection of the transformation that is supposed to take place in each individual. This process, called Teshuvah or repentance, is a gradual cleansing of the soul. Our calendar does not demand this cycle in mere minutes; it provides a month and a half, a long period of reflection beginning with the month of Elul.[10] In Ashkenazic tradition, the shofar is blown every morning during the month of Elul to awaken the Jewish soul to repentance. Rosh Hashanah is another clarion call to wake up and change ourselves and our fate for the better.[14] For God's judgment is not yet set in stone, and we can still affect His decision. From the Rosh Hashanah table to the Yom Kippur desert, the proper observance of the month of Tishrei is a reaffirmation of commitment to both God and the Jewish community.

Tishrei is a time of renewal, physically and spiritually. The old year ends, and a new year begins; the seasons turn, and in Israel the rains begin. The foods associated with the month of Tishrei symbolize that feeling of renewal in both body and spirit, and the hopes that all of Israel hold for a good new year.

POMEGRANATE: SYMBOL OF TESHUVAH

Pomegranates have an hard, bitter shell which is inedible; inside, they're bursting with juicy seeds. The difference between the inner and outer substance of the fruit symbolizes the act of Teshuvah. The hard shell of the pomegranate is like the soul of the person before Teshuvah. The habitual sinner doesn't feel the need to change. He builds a hard shell around his heart, convincing himself that he hasn't done anything wrong, that there is no reason to repent. To do teshuvah, he must break this barrier of indifference and create a softer core, a soul responsive to God and His words. The reformed sinner has cut through the tough outside and reached the soft seeds inside the fruit.

In Midrashic and Talmudic sources, the pomegranate's many seeds symbolize blessing and plenty. For example, in the Babylonian Talmud, Berachot 57a, Rabbi Hiyya the son of Abba discusses the significance of different fruits in a dream. Of the fruits mentioned, small pomegranates are said to signify a fruitful business, large ones an increase in one's business, and split ones a greater increase in Torah or Mitzvot (commandments).[17]

He waits until Yom Kippur to seal the third book.[11] Eliyahu Ki Tov states in the name of Maimonides[12] that during the entire year, one should see oneself as half meritorious and half guilty (and thus, neither righteous nor evil.)[13]

OF THE SEVEN SPECIES

Pomegranates are named in the Torah as one of the seven species of Israel. The seven species (wheat, barley, grapes [wine], figs, pomegranates, olives [oil] and dates[15]) are traditionally eaten on Tu B'Shevat, the New Year of the trees, to celebrate the fertility of the trees and the land of Israel (See Shevat chapter).

WHEN SINS ARE IGNORED

Rav Huna says that when a man sins repeatedly, that sin becomes permissible for him. The Rabbis ask if one could actually think it becomes permissible for him? The Talmud answers: No, it means he begins to think it permissible.[16]

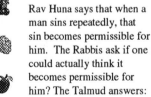

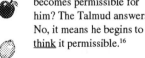

Pomegranates also symbolize the wealth of Torah in the Jewish people. For instance, at the end of the aforementioned passage, the Talmud uses a verse in Song of Songs[18] as proof that even the illiterate in Israel are full of good deeds as a pomegranate is full of seeds. Another passage, in Song of Songs Rabbah, compares pomegranate seeds to children studying Torah.[19] The children sit neat and orderly, in rows, like pomegranate seeds. The Jewish children are being praised in two ways. Like pomegranate seeds, they are numerous. However, because they sit neatly in rows, they are also attentive; all their concentration is on their studies. They _want_ to learn Torah. In these passages, the fruit is used to convey a blessed state, where our people, young and old, learned and unlearned, are dedicated to Torah and to Jewish learning.

WATER ON SUCCOT
NISUCH HAMAYIM- THE WATER LIBATION

Most people know of water on Tishrei as it relates to the custom of Tashlich. On the afternoon of the first day of Rosh Hashanah, we journey to a free-flowing body of water and recite the last three lines of Micah and other prayers. We also throw breadcrumbs into the water, symbolizing the throwing away of our sins.

Water was also a major element of the service at the Holy Temple on Succot, the Festival of Booths. Every sacrifice included a flour-offering

Tashlich can be done on the second day of Rosh Hashanah if the first day falls on Shabbos,[20] or if one could not (for a very good reason) make Tashlich on the first day.

Some people actually empty their pockets of breadcrumbs.

The word _Tashlich_ means "you shall throw," and the custom is based on Micah 7:19, "He shall return and grant us compassion; He shall hide our iniquities _and you shall cast into the depths of the sea all their sins._"[21]

covered in oil, and wine, which was poured on
the altar. (Generally, the word *"nesech"* or
"libation" in the Torah refers to the wine.) But
during Succot, an extra libation was added;
water was poured on the *tamid* (daily) sacrifice
in the morning. This libation, known as *nisuch
hamayim* (the pouring of the waters), was
accompanied by a joyous, intense celebration.[22]

These festivities, known as Simchat Beit
Hashoevah (the Rejoicing at the Place of the
Water Drawing), are described in the Talmud
as the epitome of happiness. In Tractate Sukah,
it is written, "He who has not seen the rejoicing
at the place of the water-drawing has never
seen rejoicing in his life."[23] As the waters were
poured, the people broke out in music and
song, except on the Sabbath and the first day of
Succot.[24]

Since the burning of the Holy Temple, we no
longer sacrifice or do the libations. But we can
learn much from the meaning of Nisuch
Hamayim, whose waters symbolized the waters
of creation,[25] and their purity was a reflection
of the state achieved through repentance. They
were drawn from the pool of Siloan or Shiloach
in the city of David (outside the present wall of
Jerusalem).[26] The Shiloach was called 'the Well
of Salvation,' since by tradition, the kings of
the House of David were anointed over the
Shiloach, and through these kings, salvation
came to Israel. The cool, clear waters of the
Shiloach symbolized the salvation that God
grants His people during Tishrei. So those
visiting the Temple on Succot saw the joy of a

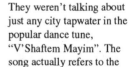

MAYIM-MAYIM!

They weren't talking about
just any city tapwater in the
popular dance tune,
"V'Shaftem Mayim". The
song actually refers to the
Shiloach! The words,
"V'shaftem mayim vesason
mima'aynei hayeshua,"[27]
mean: "Therefore with joy
shall you draw water out of
the wells of salvation."[28]

6

people who were assured of deliverance in the year to come.[29]

SUCCOT: RAIN OF BLESSING

Succot is the beginning of the rainy season in Israel; we mark this time with two special prayers for the coming of the rains.

From Shemini Azeret (the eighth day of Succot) until the second day of Passover, Jews all around the world say "Mashiv Haruach Umorid Hagashem- May the Winds Blow and the Rain Fall", before the second blessing in the Shemonah Esrai.

In an Orthodox synagogue, the Cantor or prayer leader recites a longer, communal prayer for rain on Shemini Azeret. This public prayer serves two purposes. First, it initiates the change in liturgy. Second, as Succot is the festival in which God passes judgment over water, and in which He decides how much rain will fall,[33] the Cantor is petitioning God for a good amount of rain in the coming year. His prayer might make the difference between famine and feast for the community.

The question of bread or starvation is the key to the concept of water in Tishrei. Water is the nourishment on which man survives; lack of water will mean a year of hardship, and a struggling community does not have the time or the resources to devote itself to Torah. Rainwater is a sign of God's pleasure or displeasure, the key to the revitalization of the earth. Just as the Jewish community awakens

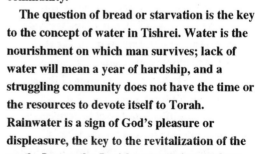

spiritually, its members pray for the water which will help the harvest.

In biblical times, our people were deeply connected to the land; as part of an agricultural society, every Jew knew the importance of the prayer for rain. Even after the destruction of the Second Temple, when Jews often bought their grain or bread from gentile farmers and bakers, it was still a matter of local concern: Would the town's produce be enough to feed everyone? But today, in our technologically oriented society, it's harder to appreciate the importance of water as a force of growth. So how do we achieve a real connection to the prayer for rain? We can realize that somewhere down the line, the food we purchase at a supermarket is dependent on a seasonal cycle of rain. Thus, though the prayer is based on the Israeli agricultural cycle, it attains global significance.

According to Eliyahu Ki Tov, author of *The Book of Our Heritage,* it would have been proper to say this prayer on the first day of Succot, just as we say the prayer for dew on the first day of Passover. Instead, we wait until Shemini Azeret, the eighth day of the festival, for two reasons. First, rain would make it impossible to observe the commandment of eating in the sukah. Second, in biblical times, there was the additional problem that rain would make it difficult to travel to Jerusalem and return (a requirement for the festival).[37]

While the Rabbis wished the rain to fall in its proper time,[39] they were also concerned with

FLOUR AND BASIC SURVIVAL

Flour is seen as a subsistence food, whose lack makes the study of Torah difficult, if not impossible. Our sages said, *"Im ain kemach, ain Torah"*[34]— if there's no flour, there's no Torah. Together, flour and water become bread, a major food staple.

RAIN AND JUDGMENT

God's judgment on rain is part of an agreement He made with us when we accepted the mitzvot. In Israel, rain comes only if we've been good; if we've sinned, the skies are shut,[35] and only prayer or fasting (in other words, Teshuvah) may open them. In Talmudic times, it was not uncommon for communities to establish fast days in response to a drought.

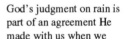

THE THREE FESTIVALS: AN AGRICULTURAL CYCLE

The prayer for dew is recited on Passover because God judges produce on Passover and the crops need dew.[36] The three major festivals (Passover, Shavuot, the Festival of Weeks, and Succot) thus follow the agricultural calendar. Shavuot is known as the holiday of the harvest— the first fruits of the seven species are brought as an offering to the Temple; the rest of the produce is cut and left in the fields to dry.[38]

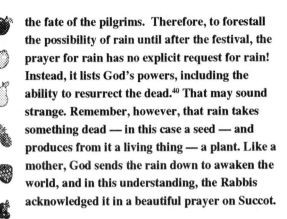

the fate of the pilgrims. Therefore, to forestall the possibility of rain until after the festival, the prayer for rain has no explicit request for rain! Instead, it lists God's powers, including the ability to resurrect the dead.[40] That may sound strange. Remember, however, that rain takes something dead — in this case a seed — and produces from it a living thing — a plant. Like a mother, God sends the rain down to awaken the world, and in this understanding, the Rabbis acknowledged it in a beautiful prayer on Succot.

THE ESROG

Every year we may pay exorbitant prices for a beautiful esrog or citron, one of the four species that are used in the ritual, and are shaken together throughout Succot. When the holiday ends, most people throw out their still-sweet esrog, wasting a fruit they've barely used! The following recipe, for Esrog Jam, is one answer to the pressing problem of leftover esrogim.

ESROG EINGEMACHTS
By Rebbetzin Channah Margolis

This recipe was collected by my friend Mordechai Housman. It's based on a famous, traditional recipe used by most "Yerushalmi Veiber"— Jerusalem wives of the Haredi (Black Hat) persuasion. However, they never boiled out the bitter taste of the citron. Rebbetzin Margolis did a lot of experimenting, and perfected this process.

"Esrog Eingemachts" has only two real ingredients: esrog and sugar. However, due to the extremely bitter taste of the citron fruit, the esrog must be purged of this pungent, overpowering flavor. This is no easy process. Slice (do not peel) the esrogim, and soak the pieces in a pan of water for 24 hours. Strain the esrog, discarding the water. Soak the pieces for another 24 hours, and discard the water.

Fill up a pot or pan with cold water, and put in the pieces of esrog. Bring the water to a boil, take it off the fire, and strain out the water. Fill it up again with water, and repeat this process. Do this a total of FOUR times.

Now you're ready to cook "Esrog Eingemachts". Put in just a little bit of water (not enough to cover the esrog pieces.) Add sugar, about one part to two parts of esrog. (i.e. about one cup of sugar for every two cups of esrog.) Cook over a low flame until the color changes to the color and consistency of jam (between one and two hours).

FOOD ON ROSH HASHANAH

Apples	Honey	Challah	Gourds
Carrots	Tzimmes	Leeks	Spinach
Dates	Sheep's Head	Chicken	Fish
Meat	Black-EyedPeas	Raisin Challah	Kreplach
(Lack of) Nuts			

"May it be Your Will":
The Concept of Y'hi Ratzon

On Rosh Hashanah, it's customary to say blessings beginning with the words *Y'hi Ratzon* (May it be your will...) over a variety of foods, in the hope that God will grant us a year filled with good things.[41] The wording of the *y'hi ratzon* will vary based on what food is being eaten.

The Rosh Hashanah feast begins with a blessing on challah dipped in honey, and then on apples dipped in honey: "May it be Your will, Hashem, our God and the God of our forefathers, that You renew for us a good and sweet year."[42] Honey is clearly a sweet food and easily relates to the blessing. But why specifically challah and apples? In his book *Ziv Haminhagim*, Rabbi Yehuda Dov Zinger[43] writes that the custom of eating challah and honey is connected with the juxtaposition of wheat (i.e. challah) and honey in Psalms 81:17, "And He would feed him with the cream of the wheat, and from a rock I would sate you with honey."[44] The passage refers to a future time of peace for Israel, where her enemies will eat wheat but she will eat honey. By dipping challah into honey, we convey the hopes we have for a year of tranquility.

The use of the apple on Rosh Hashanah is based on Genesis 27:27, in which Isaac says about Jacob, "See, the fragrance of my son is like the fragrance of a field which Hashem has blessed..." The Babylonian Talmud, Tractate Ta'anit 29b, identifies this fragrance as the smell of a field of apple trees.[45] Thus, the aroma of apples symbolizes the gift that we hope God will bestow, just as he gave Jacob to Isaac.

Many of the special foods used for the *y'hi ratzons* are selected not because of their "good" qualities, but because their names presage hope for the coming year. It is often a matter of wordplay and punning. For instance, it is customary to eat black-eyed peas (*rubia* in Yiddish), with the blessing "... that our merits increase" because of the similarities between *rubia* and the Hebrew word *yirbu* (increase). Another example: Leeks or cabbage, otherwise known as *karti*, are tied to the blessing "...that our enemies be decimated" because *yichr'tu* (decimated) and *karti* sound so much alike.[47]

One of the most interesting *Y'hi ratzons* involves eating a sheep's head or ram's head,[48] and reciting "May it be Your will.... that we be as the head and not as the tail."[49] In this prayer, we express the hope that in the coming year, we will be on top, strong and in control. The wordplay here is fourfold. First, the head houses the brain, which controls the rest of the body. Second, it contains the eyes, which enable a being to perceive the world around it. "Head" also connotes a leader: the head of a company or a state. Finally, in Hebrew, the word <u>head</u> or <u>*rosh*</u> is the same word used for the New Year (Rosh Hashanah, the head of the year).

However, the specific use of a sheep's or ram's head adds an allusion to the sacrifice of Isaac.[51] This event is a reminder, for us and for God, of Abraham's willingness to go against his own beliefs and do what he thought was God's will.

Though the sheep's head is preferred, the words in the blessing "that we be as the head and not as the tail" make it possible to substitute another animal.[52] Rabbi Zinger specifically mentions using the head of a chicken or a fish.[53]

MOM'S TZIMMES

This recipe is a favorite in my family:
1 pkg. carrots
1 large, or 2 medium sweet potatoes
10 prunes (dried fruit)
1 tbsp. honey
1/3 cup orange juice
2 dashes ginger

Slice two carrots and the sweet potatoes. Cut in small pieces of prunes. Add orange juice, honey, and ginger. Add some water to cover. Bring to a boil and simmer until soft, about 30 minutes.

FOODS SWEET AND SHARP

| Meat | Honey | Tzimmes | Nuts |

Our wishes for a sweet year extend to a more general custom of eating sweet foods, such as meat and honey[54] or tzimmes.[55] One should also stay away from sharp or bitter foods.[56]

Rabbi Moshe Iserlis (known as the Ramah) mentions a custom of not eating nuts on Rosh Hashanah.[57] He gives two reasons: The first has to do with *gematria*, the study of Jewish numerical mysticism. The Hebrew name for nut (*egoz*) has the same numerical value as the Hebrew name for sin (*cheit*),[58] and on Rosh Hashanah, it makes sense to stay as far away from sin as possible. The second reason is physiological. Foods such as nuts create too much phlegm or spit, and as this can hamper prayer, one should not eat such foods on Rosh Hashanah.[59]

CARROTS AND RUBIA: BY ANY OTHER NAME...

According to the Mishnah Brurah,[46] one can also use foods whose names in other languages mean the same thing. Therefore, carrots are sometimes used in place of black-eyed peas because they are called *merin* in Yiddish, which means "we should multiply".

Carrots also symbolize prosperity because of their round shape and golden color, and *tzimmes* (carrots fried with honey, and sometimes sweet potato) is a popular Ashkenazic dish.[50]

REMINDERS OF THE FOREFATHERS

Why should Abraham's sacrifice be recalled at Rosh Hashanah? It is as if we are telling God on the Day of Judgment: Remember what Abraham did for You! How can You, Merciful Hashem, judge his descendants unfavorably? This concept, of asking God to take our forefathers' good deeds into account when He judges us, is known as *z'chut avot* or the merits of our forefathers. It's mentioned in such verses as Exodus 20:6 and Deuteronomy 5:10 ("and showing mercy unto the thousandth generation of them that love Me and keep My commandments").

RAISIN CHALLAH: ABIGAIL'S GIFT

The Ashkenazic custom of eating raisin challah is based on the story of Abigail, a Jewish heroine, and her gift of atonement. Abigail was the wife of Nabal, a wicked sheep farmer who turned away King David and his men when they asked for food.[60] Though David had protected Nabal's fields in the past[61], Nabal refused to give him food and insulted him. At this affront, David brought his men to Nabal's house to attack him. However, Abigail was as good as her husband was wicked; she met David on the road with a gift of food to appease him, to ask forgiveness for her husband. She gave David (among other treats) 100 clusters of raisins and two hundred loaves of bread. Impressed with her foresight, David agreed to spare Nabal.

Abigail's act of restitution took place on Rosh Hashanah; her husband died ten days later, on Yom Kippur.[64] We commemorate Abigail's plea for forgiveness, a sentiment that is so much a part of repentance, by eating special raisin challah on Rosh Hashanah.

KREPLACH: THE HIDDEN MOON

Kreplach, tasty meat patties wrapped in a thin layer of pastry, are specially cooked for Rosh Hashanah in many Ashkenazic homes. They symbolize something hidden, because the meat inside is camouflaged by its doughy covering.

What hidden aspect of Rosh Hashanah do kreplach signify? The holiday falls on a new

DID KING DAVID ATTACK OUT OF ANGER?

This was not a story of impetuous, misplaced anger. David was well within his rights to attack Nabal; though Saul was still the reigning king, David had already been anointed by Samuel the prophet as the next king.[62] According to our sages in the Talmud,[63] David judged Nabal to be guilty of rebellion against the king and deserving of capital punishment.

DAYS OF HIDDEN ASPECT

Kreplach are also eaten on the day before Yom Kippur and on Purim. On Yom Kippur, God hides our sins when he seals us in the book of life. I will explain the significance of kreplach on Purim in the "Hidden Foods" section of the Adar chapter.

moon, and therefore it is considered a *chag shehachodesh mitchaseh bo* or "a holiday where the month is hidden". This phrase has many meanings. Physically, the moon is very new and small, and therefore, almost invisible. In that sense, the moon itself is hidden.[65] Spiritually, our sins are covered up on Rosh Hashanah and Yom Kippur, when God grants us forgiveness.[66]

But the moon is covered up in another fashion. The celebration of the New Moon is hidden by Rosh Hashanah. The New Moon is not mentioned in the Rosh Hashanah prayers, nor was it remembered in the Temple sacrifices for the New Year. Rabbi Shimshon Bar Tzadok, known as the Tashbetz (13th century Halachist), tells a parable of a king who visits a city with his entourage. The people of the city forgot the names of the king's advisors, though he brought many with him. Similarly, although the New Moon accompanies the New Year, we do not remember the former to give greater honor to the latter, the king.[67]

The midrashim give a mystical reason for the smallness of the New Moon on Rosh Hashanah. When the Satan wishes to bring charges against us on Rosh Hashanah, God asks him to bring two witnesses. However, since the moon is hidden, he can only find one; the sun. On the Ten Days of Repentance, the Satan has his witnesses, but God can tell him that he is too late; we have already repented.[68]

As we savor our kreplach on Rosh Hashanah, or any of the special foods mentioned in this

The Satan literally means "adversary"; he's the angel created by God to challenge our free will by tempting us to do evil. According to the Midrash, the Satan was determined to make Adam sin as soon as God issued his first commandment, "You shall not eat of the Tree of Knowledge."[69]

This is the basis of the common word "satan". In our tradition, Satan is not an adversary to God; rather, he is a tool which enables us to realize our free will.

chapter, we should think of the holiness of the holiday. The moon is hidden to honor Rosh Hashanah, a king of festivals. But the idea of accepting God as the King, and of renewing ourselves—the idea of Teshuvah—are present in all of the foods on Rosh Hashanah. May we all have a sweet and spiritually uplifting New Year.

MEAT KREPLACH[70]

1 3/4 cups sifted flour
1 1/2 tsp. salt
2 eggs
3 tbsp. shortening
1/2 lb. ground beef
1 onion, grated
1/2 tsp. freshly ground black pepper
2 tbsp. parsley

Sift flour and 1/2 teaspoon of the salt onto a board. Make a well in the center and place the eggs in it. Work in the flour until a dough is formed. Knead until smooth and elastic. Roll out as thin as possible. Cut into 3-inch squares.

Melt the shortening in a skillet. Add the beef, onion, pepper, parsley, and remaining salt. Saute for 10 minutes, stirring frequently. Let cool for 15 minutes.

Place 1 tablespoon of the beef mixture on each square. Fold the dough over the filling to form a triangle. Press the edges together firmly.

Drop into salted boiling water or soup. Cook for 20 minutes. If cooked in water, drain well and serve with meat dishes. If cooked in soup, serve several in each portion of soup.

For more Tishrei Recipes, see Recipe Reference Section end pages.

CHESHVAN
(Oct.- Nov.)

Torah Counting: Eighth month
Regular Counting: Second month

Foods: Potatoes   Potato Soup   Schav
Borsht (Beet Soup)

Themes: Mar-cheshvan and Bul
The Death of Rachel
Potato: Winter food
The Fast of BaHaB

"*MAR-CHESHVAN*": BITTER COLD

Winter winds... rains pouring down. Cheshvan is called "*mar-cheshvan*," <u>bitter</u> cheshvan, and not just because of the cold, autumn weather. The main theme of this month is rain; the most basic reason for the name Mar-cheshvan comes from the prefix "*mar*" meaning <u>drop</u>, as in <u>raindrop</u>. It refers to the winter rains, which begin at this time.[3]

There are no holidays in Cheshvan to sweeten the month. Several bitter things happened to our people during Cheshvan as well.

BUL: SCRIPTURAL NAME

In I Kings, 6:38, Cheshvan is given the name *Bul* from the Hebrew root *naval*, meaning wither or decay. In Cheshvan, the leaves on the trees have already begun to wither and fall.[1] The grasses also wither, and we mix in (*bolel*) food from the house to feed the animals.[2] But Radak thinks that the root of "*bul*" is "*mabul*," or flood. For this is when the rains start pouring down like a flood, on the very month that the Flood began.[4]

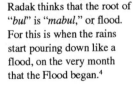

A few examples: Jereboam I (King of Israel) initiated a new festival on the fifteenth of Cheshvan, bringing divine wrath on Israel.[5] On the fifth of Cheshvan, the Chaldeans slaughtered King Tzidkiyahu's five sons before his eyes, and then blinded him. And according to Torah tradition, the Flood came during Cheshvan.[6]

OH, FOR A FESTIVAL!

Cheshvan should have had a holiday, to commemorate the building of the first Temple. As it says in I Kings 6:38, the Temple was completed on the eleventh of Cheshvan; however, Solomon the Wise waited eleven months for God to command him to dedicate it. (Though the building was completed, it was not dedicated until Tishrei!) Cheshvan missed out on its festival, and Tishrei received three. But, Cheshvan still retains the honor of the completion of the first Temple, and in the future, it will be repaid with a festival of its own.[7]

POTATO: STAPLE OF WINTER

There are no foods related, biblically or traditionally, to Cheshvan. However, as Cheshvan is the beginning of the fall and winter rains, it seemed appropriate to bring up the potato, a food which grows underground in the fall.

The potato is not Middle-Eastern; it originated in South America, and was brought to Europe by Spanish explorers, possibly as early as 1550.

This is similar to what happened with the Tabernacle, which was finished by the twenty-fifth of Kislev, but was not dedicated until the first of Nisan. (See chapter on Kislev.)

WHY DID GOD WAIT UNTIL TISHREI? It seems to me that Tishrei's plethora of holidays makes it an ideal time to dedicate the Temple. And the people were all due in Jerusalem for Sukkot, anyway, which made it an extremely convenient time.

Potatoes: Earth Food

While the stems and leaves of the potato plant are above ground, the potato itself (called a tuber) is hidden, growing from underground stems, warm and snug in the earth. The plant grows until the tuber matures, or until the first frost.

Potatoes became popular in Ireland and England. When our people settled in Eastern Europe, in Poland and Lithuania, Romania and Russia, the potato became a staple of Ashkenazic cooking.[8] Potato latkes are a traditional fried food on Chanukah (see fried foods in Kislev); potato kugel is standard fare in Ashkenazic homes on Friday nights. Potatoes have warmed many a heart during the bitter Eastern European winters. They were so popular that there is even a Yiddish folk song about them, titled, Boolbis (Potatoes).

Potatoes are from the nightshade family, but they're far from poisonous. 80% water and 20% solid, the potato contains starch (about 85% of that solid matter), protein, and vitamins and minerals.[9] No wonder this vegetable is so popular- in french fries, fluffy mashed potatoes, crisp potato chips, or potato latkes and kugel, it has become a major part of American Jewish cookery.

BOOLBIS*

Zun-tik boolbis! Moontik boolbis! Dinstich oon Mitvach-Boolbis!

Du-ner-shtich oon Frei-tig-bool-bis! Shabbos in a no-ve-neh, a

bool-beh ku-ga-leh! Zun-tik Vai-ter bool-bis!

YIDDISH

Zuntik- boolbis!
Moontik- boolbis!
Dinstich oon mitvach- boolbis!
Dunershtich oon Freitig-boolbis!
Shabbos in a noveneh, a boolbeh kugaleh!
Zuntik- Vaiter boolbis!
Uhber, boolbis.
Vaiter, boolbis.
Nuch a mul un vider, boolbis.
Haint un maurgen, boolbis.
Shabbos nuchin tshulent- a boolbeh kugaleh!
Zuntik- Vaiter boolbis.

Sunday- potatoes!
Monday- potatoes!
Tuesday and Wednesday-potatoes!
Thursday and Friday-potatoes!
For a change on Shabbos-a kugel of potatoes!
Sunday- Again potatoes!
Nothing but potatoes!
Still more potatoes!
Again and again potatoes!
Night and morning potatoes!
Shabbos after tscholent-a potato kugaleh!
Sunday again potatoes!

* The words are from Uriel Weinreich's _College Yiddish_, YIVO Institute for Jewish Research. Transliteration and translation by Toby Solomon.

18

Broit mit boolbis,	Bread with potatoes,
Fish mit boolbis.	Fish with potatoes,
Varems oon vetshereh, boolbis!	Dinner and supper, potatoes!
Uhber oon vider, boolbis.	Still and again potatoes!
Shabbos nuchin tscholent-a boolbeh kugaleh!	Shabbos after tscholent-a potato kugaleh!
Zuntik vaiter boolbis.	Sunday again potatoes.

POTATO-NIK[10]
by Anne Schevelowitz

1 pkg. dry yeast
1/8 cup lukewarm water
4 lbs. large potatoes
salt and pepper, to taste

2 cups flour
1/4 cup oil
4 eggs

Dissolve yeast in the water. Peel and grate the potatoes; add them to the yeast mixture, together with the eggs and 1 cup of flour. Mix well. Cover with remaining flour (to prevent potatoes from turning black). Let rise until double in size.

Add oil, pepper and salt; mix in the flour from the top. Pour mixture into a well-oiled 13 * 9" pan. Allow to rise again. Bake in preheated 400° oven for 1 hour.

Remove from oven immediately and turn out of pan. Serve cold, plain or with gefilte fish.

A DEATH IN THE FAMILY

The 11th of Cheshvan was a day of mourning for our people, for Rachel, our biblical mother, died and was buried on that day. We thus have a tradition of praying at Rachel's gravesite, asking God for forgiveness and compassion in her name. Jacob buried her on the road to Bethlehem and not in the cave of Machpelah, with the other Matriarchs and Patriarchs; for Jacob knew that one day Rachel's children would be exiled and would pass her gravesite. As he foresaw, when they were exiled, they passed before Rachel's grave. She could not stand to see her children suffer, and wept before God, asking Him for mercy and forgiveness. God comforted her. "Refrain your voice from weeping," He said. "There is reward for your labor, and the children shall return to their boundary."[12] It is worthy to remember Rachel, whose prayers were heeded in our hour of need.

THE FAST OF BaHaB: PREVENTIVE MEDICINE

The Fast of BaHaB first occurs on the Monday, Thursday, and Monday following Rosh Hodesh Cheshvan, and happens again, after Rosh Hodesh Iyar. (BaHaB stands for the second (Beit), fifth (Hey) and second (Beit) days of the week.)

Some say that we fast at the beginning of Cheshvan to pray for the rains that come during Cheshvan. There is a second, more probable opinion, that the fast of BaHaB is a fast of atonement for sins that were committed during the previous months. Tishrei and Nisan, which

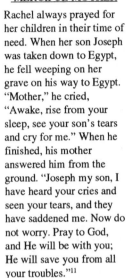

RACHEL: MERCIFUL MOTHER

Rachel always prayed for her children in their time of need. When her son Joseph was taken down to Egypt, he fell weeping on her grave on his way to Egypt. "Mother," he cried, "Awake, rise from your sleep, see your son's tears and cry for me." When he finished, his mother answered him from the ground. "Joseph my son, I have heard your cries and seen your tears, and they have saddened me. Now do not worry. Pray to God, and He will be with you; He will save you from all your troubles."[11]

RACHEL'S PRAYERS

When Menasseh, King of Israel placed idols in the Temple, God was very angry and wanted to destroy us. The Patriarchs prayed for us and none of their prayers were heeded. Sarah, Rebbeca, Leah and Miriam pleaded for their children, and they were not answered. Moses our Teacher prayed, and his prayers could not break through the heavenly gates. Then Rachel stepped up. "Lord," she said, "Whose mercy is greater, Yours or a human being's? I let my rival into my house. When my sister Leah replaced me

20

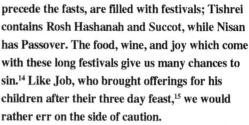

on my wedding night, I kept silent. I even gave my sister the signs that Jacob and I had established, to save her from embarrassment. Why, then, won't You be silent for the sake of Your children?" God answered her, "You have made a righteous defense. You are rewarded for giving the signs to your sister; I shall be silent."[13]

WHY IS THERE NO FAST OF BaHaB AFTER SHAVUOT? Shavuot is a one-day holiday and would presumably not give us much chance to sin.[16]

precede the fasts, are filled with festivals; Tishrei contains Rosh Hashanah and Succot, while Nisan has Passover. The food, wine, and joy which come with these long festivals give us many chances to sin.[14] Like Job, who brought offerings for his children after their three day feast,[15] we would rather err on the side of caution.

RECIPES FOR CHESHVAN

The following recipes will bring a taste of Autumn to your meal. Potato soup and borscht (beet soup) add the yellow, brown and red of Fall leaves. And being soups, they symbolize the rain that falls during Cheshvan. Schav, a soup of sorrel or sour grass, adds a touch of green, a reminder that Winter has not yet come.

RATNER'S WORLD FAMOUS POTATO SOUP[17*]

6 potatoes, peeled and quartered
1/2 cup diced carrots
1/2 cup chopped green pepper
1/2 cup tomato juice
2 tbsp. salt
1 tbsp. chopped dill
1/2 cup flour

3 onions, sliced
1/2 cup chopped celery
1/2 cup chopped parsley
2 quarts water
1/2 cup onions, baked in clarified butter
1/2 cup Clarified Butter

In a large kettle, combine potatoes, onions, carrots, celery, green pepper, parsley, tomato juice, water, and salt. Bring to a boil, lower heat and simmer covered, for 40 minutes. Stir in baked onions and dill. Blend thoroughly.

In a small skillet, heat butter. Add flour and stir over medium heat until flour is golden brown. Gradually add 1 cup of the hot soup to the flour mixture, stirring constantly.

Stir the flour mixture into the remaining soup.

Cook, stirring, over low heat until soup bubbles and thickens. Taste and add what you wish.

Serve piping hot to eight people.
* Note: This soup may not taste exactly like Ratner's potato soup, as I have not included their recipe for clarified butter and baked onions.

BORSCHT (BEET SOUP)[18]

2 bunches beets, peeled and grated
3 quarts water
2 tbsp salt
2 tsp sour salt or juice of 1 medium lemon
3/4 cup sugar
boiled potato and sour cream (optional)

Place all your ingredients in a large kettle. Bring to a boil and simmer for 20 minutes, or until beets are tender. Taste the soup, and add seasonings as you like them.

Serve hot or cold with a boiled potato or sour cream to eight or ten people.

SCHAV [19]

1 1/2 lbs. sorrel (sour grass) *
1 quart water (can use spring water)
1/3 cup sugar
1 tbsp vinegar
2 tbsp lemon juice
1 tsp salt
2 eggs beaten lite and thick
1/2 cup sour cream

Wash sorrel leaves, remove stems, chop fine. Put sorrel, water and sugar in a 2-quart pot; bring to a boil, lower heat, and cook gently for 10 minutes. Add vinegar, lemon juice and salt. Cool. Mix eggs and sour cream until blended. Add to the Schav and mix thoroughly. Chill and serve cold. (Makes 1-1/2 quarts of soup.)

* Some recipes suggest Swiss chard instead of sorrel leaves.

KISLEV
(NOV.-DEC.)

Torah Counting: Ninth Month
Regular Counting: Third Month

Themes: Miracles: Remember the Flask of Oil
The Dedication of the Tabernacle
The Rededication of the Temple
Women and Chanukah

THE TWENTY-FIFTH OF KISLEV: A DAY OF SANCTIFICATION

The Maccabees were not the first to witness a *kiddish Hashem* (an act which consecrates God's name) on the twenty-fifth of Kislev. The chain of sanctification started during our ancestors' sojourn through the desert, when the Tabernacle was finished on the twenty-fourth of Kislev. It would have been dedicated on the next day, but God delayed the event until Rosh Chodesh Nisan, to mix the joy of the Tabernacle with

Foods: Olive oil Milk Wine Cheese Cake
Fried foods: Latkes Sufganiyot Loukomades Zelebi

KISLEV: DEDICATION TO TORAH

Latkes and Sufganiyot, cheese blintzes and sour cream. These are the norm in Ashkenazic homes at the end of Kislev, when we light our Chanukah menorahs. And the story of the Hasmoneans, the courageous priests who fought for our right to worship God in our own land, is the story of Kislev: the month devoted to Jewish education and rededication of one's self to God and Torah.

During Kislev, the first covenant between God and man was created. On Rosh Chodesh Kislev,

God showed Noah the first rainbow as a promise that He would never again flood the world. Noah's part of the agreement happened two days earlier, when he exited the ark on the twenty-eighth of Cheshvan. Noah brought sacrifices of thanksgiving to God and pledged to follow God's laws (the seven laws of the sons of Noah). God then rewarded Noah for his faithfulness with a blessing, permission to eat meat, and a prohibition against killing humans. The sign of the rainbow was a symbol of this pact of peace. Thus, Kislev's sign is the rainbow, which also represents the mixed sunshine and rain that is typical of this month.[3]

OLIVE OIL: PURE LIGHT, BURNING BRIGHT

Olive oil is <u>the item</u> this month because of its symbolism and its role in Jewish history. It was used in the Tabernacle and also in the Holy Temple as fuel for the menorah, the six-branched candelabra that was lit daily by the Kohen Gadol (High Priest) (See next page: "The Menorah: When Was It Lit?") But why olive oil and not sesame oil, or vegetable oil, or another variety? Olive oil burns hotter and brighter than other oils, producing a clean glow. The Midrash Tanhuma, Tetsaveh, §3, remarks on the pressed olive oil used in the menorah; Rabbi Hanina Sgan Kohanim says that once when he was in the Holy Temple, the menorah was lit on Rosh Hashanah, and remained lit the entire year. The light of the

Isaac's birth and the Exodus. God owed us a celebration in Kislev, so He gave us Chanukah.[1]

And in Hagai 2, it describes our delight when we finished building the foundations of the Second Temple—also on the twenty-fourth of Kislev. On the next night, we exalted in the simchah of the foundations.[2]

OLIVE OIL: ITS SPECIAL QUALITIES

The Midrash and Talmud detail some of the more miraculous and enlightening facts about the olive oil used in the Temple.

Olive oil is a symbol of light to the world;[4] when Noah sent the dove out to scout the flooded earth, the bird returned with an olive branch, a sign that the floodwaters had receded, and that there was once more light in the world.[5]

Olive oil is not so simple to make. According to Maimonides, it took the Hasmoneans eight days to make new pure olive oil for the menorah.[6] Our ancestors would harvest the olives three times because the olive tree ripens gradually, in three shifts. And for each harvest, they would process three different types of oil. So there are actually nine kinds of olive oil.[7] The oil used for the menorah was the first squeezing of the first olive picking, and it was considered the purest.[8]

Consider the pounding the olive needs to yield the drops of rich oil locked inside that small fruit. We see ourselves as having been pounded and physically persecuted throughout history. In the end, when we repent and pray to God, we too will yield our "oil"— for God will answer our prayers. And so we are compared to an olive tree in Jeremiah 11:16: "The Lord called thy name, a leafy olive-tree, fair with goodly fruit...".[11]

Jeremiah also compared our ancestors to olive oil, for just as oil does not mix with other liquids, we do not intermarry; and like oil, we rise in stature when we follow God's command-ments.[12]

THE MENORAH: WHEN WAS IT LIT?

Our sages express two opinions; Rashi and most authorities state that the Menorah was lit only at night. In the morning the Priests would clean it out and put in fresh wicks and oil, and check that the Ner

menorah symbolized the light of God shining in the world; the midrash states that it illuminated every courtyard in Jerusalem, and all could use it.[9] In fact, while most houses had windows wider on the inside to admit more light, the windows of the Holy Temple were wider on the outside so as to emit more of God's light into the world.[10] Thus, the menorah's olive oil is very much connected with Kislev's theme of service and dedication to God.

Several hundred years later, the symbolism of olive oil and of the Menorah figure in an event of spiritual redemption. In about 165 B.C.E., on the twenty-fifth of Kislev, the Hasmoneans, victorious in their war against the Syrian-Greeks, liberated the Holy Temple in Jerusalem. Their first act after purifying and rededicating the Temple was to try to light the menorah. However, they could not find any oil for fuel, for their enemies had made the flasks of olive oil impure. Fortunately, they discovered one flask of pure olive oil whose seal had not been broken; they used that oil to light the menorah. That single flask, which should have lasted for one day, burned instead for eight days—enough time for the Hasmoneans to prepare a fresh supply of oil.[15]

But what was the importance of relighting the menorah? In the Chanukah story, the war against the Syrian-Greeks was not, as some would think, a simple question of control of the land of Israel. The Hasmoneans, a family of priests from the village of Modi'in, were actually fighting for the very survival of Judaism. In about 168 B.C.E., Antiochus Epiphanes, the Seleucid ruler who was at that point in control of Israel, declared a war against the Jewish religion. Practicing Judaism was forbidden on pain of death. An idol was erected on the altar in the Holy Temple, and on the twenty-fifth of Kislev, pagan sacrifices were offered. The Hasmoneans rose up against the Syrian-Greek tyranny, and after a pitched three-year campaign, liberated the Temple Mount.

Antiochus' oppression of the Jews was the culmination of the Seleucid struggle to Hellenize the Jewish population. The Greeks and their supporters saw nothing wrong with accepting other peoples' gods; some of the Jewish population (mostly the upper class) were sympathetic to Hellenism, but there remained a core of devout Jews who refused to assimilate.[20] When Judah the Maccabee and his brothers lit the Menorah on the twenty-fifth of Kislev, fully three years after Antiochus' original decree, the light of that olive oil did not just signify the continuation of the Temple service; it also symbolized the continuation of the vibrant flame of Judaism, the light that was almost extinguished.

FRIED FOODS AND CHANUKAH: A RICH TRADITION

| Latkes | Sufganiyot | Loukomades | Zelebi |

We commemorate the miracle of the flask of oil on Chanukah with a tradition of eating fried treats. The names and shapes of these delica-

Tamid (the Eternal Flame) was still burning (see sidebar on the Ner Tamid). Then they would light the Menorah again the next night.[13] Maimonides, however, claims that the Menorah was lit both morning and night, and burned constantly.[14]

THE *NER TAMID*: SOULS IN THE FLAME

The Ner Tamid (Eternal Flame) was one of the lights of the Menorah; according to Rashi, it burned continuously on its own until Simon the Righteous died, circa 312 B.C.E.[16] Every morning, the Priests would check that the Ner Tamid was still lit. When the flame stopped, the Priests re-lit it.[17]

Why would God need the light of the Eternal Flame? It is interpreted thus: The light was put in God's house for our sake, not His. This candle is symbolic of the protection and atonement that God grants us when we fulfill His commandments. For the soul is compared to a candle: "*Ki ner Hashem nishmat adam*—for the candle of God is the soul of mankind."[18] God is always watching over us, just as the Ner Tamid was always burning in the Tabernacle and the Holy Temple.[19]

And in Midrash Tanhuma, Tetsaveh, §8, God said to Moses, "Tell my people that in this world, they needed the light of the Ner Tamid, the Eternal Flame. But in the next world, I will give you a new candle (the Messiah) in the merit of this light."

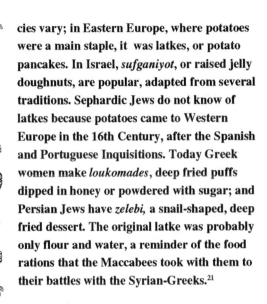

cies vary; in Eastern Europe, where potatoes were a main staple, it was latkes, or potato pancakes. In Israel, *sufganiyot*, or raised jelly doughnuts, are popular, adapted from several traditions. Sephardic Jews do not know of latkes because potatoes came to Western Europe in the 16th Century, after the Spanish and Portuguese Inquisitions. Today Greek women make *loukomades*, deep fried puffs dipped in honey or powdered with sugar; and Persian Jews have *zelebi,* a snail-shaped, deep fried dessert. The original latke was probably only flour and water, a reminder of the food rations that the Maccabees took with them to their battles with the Syrian-Greeks.[21]

WOMEN AND CHANUKAH

We women have a special stake in the miracle of Chanukah. Judah and his Hasmonean brothers had help in the battle against the Syrian Greeks; the Midrash and Talmud mention several different women who either fought for Judaism or martyred themselves to keep the Torah in this period of hardship. Women were deeply affected by Antiochus' rule, which often targeted the Jewish laws of marriage and modesty (*tzniut*); i.e., one decree forced an engaged woman to consort with the king's officer before she was allowed to marry her intended. Our role in the Chanukah story is so profound that it is customary for women to abstain from work for the first half hour that the Chanukah candles

27

are lit. Some Sephardic families prohibit women from working the whole of Chanukah, or on the first and last day of the holiday.[22]

Who were these courageous women of Chanukah? The tales cited in the Midrash are often ambiguous; the same story is told in several sources, and these midrashim generally do not agree on the identity of the woman involved. Usually, the heroine is a daughter of an important figure, such as Mattathias or Yochanan the High Priest. Here are some of these tales:

THE ANGRY BRIDE: CATALYST FOR A REVOLT[23]

Who:

The daughter of Yochanan the High Priest

Hannah, daughter of Mattathias

When the Greeks occupied our land, in days of old, the daughters of Israel were beset by a cruel and heartless decree. Every Jewish woman who was about to marry was forced, by law, to give herself first to the Greek official of her district. This lasted for three years and eight months, until one act of an important Hasmonean bride. All the elders and the wise men of our people came to see her wed, for her father was a great man in Israel. When she was carried in her litter to the wedding feast, she stood up, removed her head covering, and tore off her dress until she stood revealed before the elders, her father, her husband, her brothers, and the common people.

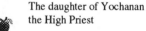

THE ANGRY BRIDE: VARIATIONS

In one version of this story, the bride is actually being taken to the palace of the Greek official when she speaks up. The brothers then take her, singing and dancing, before the Greek official, who is so delighted that he honors them with a private audience. Then, the brothers kill him and all his advisors.

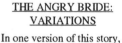

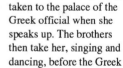

Her brothers were angry and ashamed, and would have killed her for her act of immodesty, but she addressed them thus: "I stand

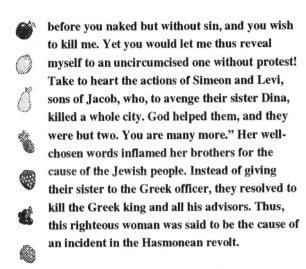

before you naked but without sin, and you wish to kill me. Yet you would let me thus reveal myself to an uncircumcised one without protest! Take to heart the actions of Simeon and Levi, sons of Jacob, who, to avenge their sister Dina, killed a whole city. God helped them, and they were but two. You are many more." Her well-chosen words inflamed her brothers for the cause of the Jewish people. Instead of giving their sister to the Greek officer, they resolved to kill the Greek king and all his advisors. Thus, this righteous woman was said to be the cause of an incident in the Hasmonean revolt.

THE BRIDE VICTIM: HAPLESS INSTIGATOR[24]

Let us all bemoan the fate of the daughter of Mattathias. On her wedding night, she was taken by a Greek officer, who coveted her for her beauty. He raped her in the Holy Temple on top of a Torah scroll, and forced her Hasmonean bridegroom to watch. When he had finished, he killed her intended and poured his blood (some say he poured pig's blood) on the altar, making it impure.

When Hannah's brother Yochanan learned what had happened, he was filled with rage to avenge both the honor of his sister and the desecration of God's temple. He slipped a sword under his robe and alone entered the palace of Niknor, the Greek official ruling Israel at the time, saying, "I have come to offer you loyalty; I will do whatever you ask."

Pleased but confused by this sudden capitulation, Niknor said, "You could be lying, but I will accept your offer if you sacrifice a pig on the altar in the Holy Temple, something your people abhor. Then I'll know your change of heart is genuine."

But Yochanan replied, "I would gladly do anything your Lordship desires. There's only one problem. If word gets out that I defamed the altar, my people will stone me and kill me. I will do as you say, but first you must order everyone out of sight except for you and me, so that I can do this without fear that the news will reach my people."

Satisfied with Yochanan's words, Niknor ordered all to leave except for the two of them. Uttering a prayer to God, Yochanan plunged his sword, now revealed, into his enemy's bosom.

THE LEVITE WOMAN AND
HER CIRCUMCISED SON[25]

On the balcony she stood, she and her circumcised son, a small, eight-day old infant. But the squalling baby did not deter the Greek soldiers who would soon kill her for obeying one of the oldest laws of her people. She faced the crowd below. "Yes, I am proud to have made my son a member of our people. With trumpets and fanfare I have ushered in my son's covenant with God. Now we will go as we have lived: two children of Israel, faithful to the God of our forefathers." And with those words, she jumped from the rooftops, her son in her arms.

HANNAH AND HER SEVEN SONS[26]

This is the most famous of all stories connected with Chanukah, save perhaps for the story of Judith. Countless Midrashic and Talmudic sources have retold it (you can have some fun, if you want, and read through the variations); it was even summarized for the Ashkenazic liturgy of the first Shabbat of Chanukah![27]

The following account is a (very abbreviated) retelling of the version presented in Chanukah: Its History, Observance and Significance[28]:

In the days of Antiochus, there was a woman named Hannah who had seven sons, all God-fearing people. One day Phillip, the appointed governor of Judea, arrested Hannah and her sons, determined to enforce Antiochus' new decree. Antiochus had proclaimed: "Who ever shall not bow to my image, eat pig's meat, and reject the religion of Moses shall be killed."

Antiochus, who was on his way to Antioch but close to Jerusalem, resolved to personally witness the execution of his decree. Hannah and her sons were brought before him. He tried at first to persuade the oldest son to bow before him. When the boy proclaimed his loyalty to the Torah, Antiochus decided to make an example of him. He severed the boy's tongue, hands and feet, flayed the

Who:

Hannah (Josephus)

Unnamed (Most sources)

Miriam, Daughter of
Tanchum or Nachtum
(Eichah Rabbah and
Pesikta Rabbasi)

VARIATIONS IN HANNAH

Some sources give the king
the title *Kaisar* (Hebrew
for Caesar), suggesting that
this story happened under
one of the Roman
emperors. But the stories
are so similar to those in
Maccabbees and Josephus,
that one would assume
they refer to the same
incident.

The circumstances of
Hannah's death also
change in the retelling.
According to the Talmud,[29]
she jumped off the roof,
and a heavenly voice
proclaimed, "The mother
of the children is joyous."[30]
Eichah Rabbah relates that
she lost her sanity and
committed suicide.[31]

skin on his head, and placed the boy alive, in
front of his whole family, in a copper pot over
burning coals.

"You see?" said Antiochus to the others,
"You can be spared this. If you bow before me,
I will let you live." But the rest of Hannah's
sons followed their brother's example, and were
tortured and killed in turn.

At last Hannah stood alone over the bodies of
her dead children. And she prayed, "My mouth
opens wide against Your enemies; for they were
unable to snare my sons with their delusions or
their threats. God who is above all powers, heed
the plea of Your maidservant. Let this foe not
defile me. Show me the place You have reserved
for my sons, who died in Your name. The whole
world will praise You, as will I."

When Hannah finished praying, her soul
departed; she fell over the bodies of her sons
and lay with them.

THE WOMAN WHO KILLED THE GENERAL[32]

There is an old custom to eat cheese products
on Chanukah because of the actions of a brave
woman who killed a general (often called
Holofernes) during the Hasmonean battles after
overstuffing him with wine and cheese. The
identity of this woman is unclear. Most sources
call her Judith the widow. Eliyahu Ki Tov says
that she was the daughter of Yochanan the High
Priest, who is mentioned in other stories of
heroism, but the account below is about Judith,
not the daughter of Yochanan:

Once a Greek ruler named Holofernes besieged Jerusalem for many days. But in the city there was a wise and pious woman named Judith, a widow from an important family. When she saw what was happening, she went to the gates of Jerusalem with her maid. She said to the guards, "Let me exit the city; perhaps God will perform a miracle through me." The guards allowed her to pass, and she slipped into the enemy's camp.

She was brought before Holofernes, who was taken by her beauty and filled with lust. "Who are you," he said, "and why have you come?"

Judith smiled sweetly. "I am from a family of prophets in Israel; we have seen that the city will be given into your hands soon, for the people are sinning. I have come to ask you to spare my family."

Holofernes was so impressed by Judith's beauty and charm that he asked her to marry him. Judith answered, "This is really too great an honor for your servant; but if it be the General's desire, I will wed you. Only tell your servants not to harm two women walking by the river, for I wish first to prepare by immersing and purifying myself." Holofernes agreed, eager for his marriage bed.

That night, the General feasted with his men, and they ate cheese and drank wine until they were very tired. When his officers left for their own tents, Holofernes fell asleep in his bed, drunk and content. Judith saw her chance. With a prayer for God's help, she

JUDITH: DIFFERENCES IN THE TALE

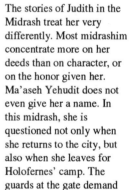

The stories of Judith in the Midrash treat her very differently. Most midrashim concentrate more on her deeds than on character, or on the honor given her. Ma'aseh Yehudit does not even give her a name. In this midrash, she is questioned not only when she returns to the city, but also when she leaves for Holofernes' camp. The guards at the gate demand to know why she wants to leave: Is she involved with a Greek soldier? Is she planning to betray the city? Both that midrash and the Midrash L'Chanukah relate the suspicion with which she is treated when she returns with the General's head. Thus, in these midrashim, Judith is not honored until she has proof of her goodness in the form of Holofernes' head.

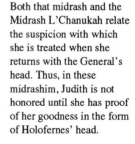

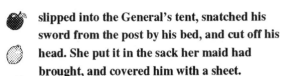

How different is Ma'aseh HaYehudit, taken from Chemdat Hayamim! This long, involved story, gives Judith a much bigger role than the preceding midrashim. She berates Uziahu the Nasi (Prince) and the priests in Jerusalem for wanting to surrender the city, and begs them to try her plan first. Under Judith's influence, Uziahu and his cohorts repent. They accompany her to the gates of the city and bless her endeavors, and they welcome her when she returns. Here Judith is a leader, respected and supported by her people. In addition, the language of this Midrash is often straight from the liturgy and from Psalms, and the tale is filled with Judith's prayers. This would date the Midrash in a later period, Mishnaic, or perhaps during the Middle Ages, when, according to Joan Nathan, food historian and author of The Jewish Holiday Kitchen, the story of Judith gained more popularity.[33]

slipped into the General's tent, snatched his sword from the post by his bed, and cut off his head. She put it in the sack her maid had brought, and covered him with a sheet.

Then the two brave women slipped down to the river and to the gates of Jerusalem. The guards were suspicious. "How do we know you have not given away secrets," they said, "or that you weren't consorting with the enemy?"

Judith said, "See for yourself: I have here the head of their General." She lifted Holofernes' head out of the sack. Seeing this, the guards opened the gates of Jerusalem with joy. The next day, the people of Jerusalem faced the enemy, and God gave them a great victory.

For Kislev Recipes, see Recipe Reference.

TEVET
(DEC.-JAN.)

Torah Counting: Tenth month
Regular Counting: Fourth month

Foods: (AVOID) Spicy Foods:
Hot Peppers, Garlic Bread, Babaganoush
(EAT) Simple Foods:
Toast, Eggs, Warm milk, Black Coffee

THEMES:The Three Fasts
The Eighth of Tevet
The Ninth of Tevet
The Tenth of Tevet: A Day of Introspection
The Festival Sacrifice Scorecard
Ceremonial Offering
Eating Before a Fast Day

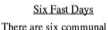
<u>Six Fast Days</u>

THE THREE FASTS

Tevet has a dubious honor: the accumula-
tion of three fast days, one following the other.
The eighth and the ninth of Tevet are held by
certain righteous people, and the tenth of
Tevet is a communal fast, one of the four
major fast days connected with the destruction
of the Holy Temple.[2]

There are six communal
fast days in the Jewish
calendar: Yom Kippur, The
Fast of Esther, The Fast of
Gedaliah, the Tenth of
Tevet, the Seventeenth of
Tammuz, and the Ninth of
Av. Yom Kippur is
mentioned in the Torah.
The Fast of Esther was
ordained by Mordechai and
Esther.[1] And the other four
were ordained by the later
prophets as a cycle; each of
these fasts commemorates
one event in the history of
the Temple's destruction.[3]

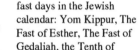
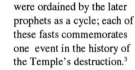

Many Hassidic stories warn against fasting more than required. They doubt the morality of men who fast from Sabbath to Sabbath, when they could be doing good deeds or reciting Psalms or studying Torah. For instance, Rabbi Hayyim of Kossov said, "A Jew, perhaps, may recite a psalm with such fervor as to incline heaven much farther than if he spent his life in fasting."[4]

Inaccurate translations have even spurred antisemitism. Consider Michaelangelo's "Moses." The artist's portrayal of a Moses with horns was based on a mistranslation of *"karan or pnei Moshe"* (Moses' face was shining) as "Moses' face had horns".[7] This may have aided the anti-semitic stereotype of the devil-Jew, already established in Christian theology.[8]

THE EIGHTH OF TEVET

Some people fast on the eighth of Tevet, in memory of the first translation of the Torah into Greek.

During the Second Temple period, on the eighth of Tevet, Ptolemy of Egypt, one of the Greek kings who succeeded Alexander of Macedonia, forced seventy-two of our Elders to translate the Torah. Instead of letting them come up with a joint translation, he placed each of them in a different room and ordered them to translate the Torah separately. He thought to make a mockery of us, but a miracle occurred which, instead, showed the Torah's divine origin. The translations emerged the same, even in places where the scholars had deviated from a literal translation.[5]

Despite this occurrence, there is an intense feeling of sadness associated with the eighth of Tevet. Our sages compare it to the day on which the Golden Calf was made. Before Ptolemy's translation, the Torah was solely in the hands of our people. A Gentile who wished to learn Torah was forced first to learn Hebrew, and to gain some knowledge of the Oral Law. The translation of the Torah into Greek made it accessible to the unlearned, and easier to mistranslate or misinterpret.[6]

THE NINTH OF TEVET

On the ninth of Tevet, our people mourned the loss of Ezra the Scribe and Nehemiah, who led us on our return from the Babylonian exile. Some commemorate their passing with a fast.[9]

THE TENTH OF TEVET: JERUSALEM IS BESIEGED

On the tenth of Tevet, during the First Temple period, Nebuchadnezzar, the King of Babylonia, began his siege of Jerusalem. This event was just the beginning of a long list of calamities that befell our people. Nebuchadnezzar's siege continued for three long years, a time of starvation and valiant defense by our people. But our sins were too great. Eventually, Nebuchadnezzar broke through the walls of Jerusalem, and captured and burned the Holy Temple, our most precious treasure.

In modern times, it is hard to understand the loss of a Temple that we have not known for thousands of years. Standing at the Kotel (Wall) in Jerusalem might awaken some of those feelings but not all are able to visit Israel for this purpose. Instead, we shall try to evoke what the Temple was like, and its meaning to us.

The Temple was the center of Jewish life for hundreds of years. Before each of the three major festivals, hundreds of people would journey to Jerusalem for the holiday's sacrifices. The Temple service was a homage to the strength and glory of God; the Levites were master singers, especially trained to evoke God's praise with their voices, their words, and their music. The Priests in the Temple executed each festival in graceful ceremonies, most of which were written down for posterity by our own sages, and by other witnesses.[11] The descriptions of these ceremonies testify to the beauty that was extinguished when the Temple was destroyed.

THE TENTH AND FRIDAY

All public fasts are delayed until Sunday if they fall on Shabbat, except for Yom Kippur. But fasts that fall on Friday are observed, even though we must enter the Sabbath fasting.[10]

FESTIVAL SACRIFICE SCORECARD

The three major festivals were pilgrimage holidays; every family was obligated to travel to Jerusalem and witness the Kohen offering, besides the normal daily sacrifices, a *Musaf* (Additional) sacrifice specific to that festival.

The *Musaf* was always an *Olah* ("Elevation Offering"), which was completely burnt and offered only to God (hence, its name.) Specified quantities of bulls, rams, and male lambs[12], all unblemished, were brought each day of the Festival.[13]

A *minchah* or "meal offering", fine flour mixed with oil,[14] accompanied the *Olah* sacrifice; each animal required a different measurement of the mixture.[15]

Other festival practices included: the Paschal, *Omer*, and *Hagigah*[17] sacrifices, offered on Passover, and Bikkurim, the gift of the first fruits, brought on Shavuot.[18]

CEREMONIAL OFFERING

The sacrifice of the Paschal lamb, done in three shifts, was only one of the hundreds of beautiful rituals performed in the Temple. This passage, quoted directly from The Book Of Our Heritage, describes the sprinkling of the blood on the altar:

"'Throughout the slaughtering and the offering, the Levites would sing the Hallel'.[19] Each time that Hallel was sung, the trumpets were sounded three times, *teki'ah, tru'ah, teki'ah*. The Kohanim stood row after row with dishes of silver and of gold in their hands. The whole of one row had silver dishes and the whole of another row had golden ones and they remained separate so that it would appear even more beautiful. These vessels were wide at the top and pointed at the bottom, so that they could not be put down on the ground, for the blood in them might congeal and be unsuitable to sprinkle on the altar.

"When the animal had been slaughtered, the Kohen would receive the blood in the vessels and hand it on to his fellow and he to the next one so that many people should have a share in the mitzvah. When it reached the Kohen who was nearest to the altar he would toss it, in one swift motion, against the base. As he received a full vessel, with one hand, he would

AN INTROSPECTIVE DAY

The tenth of Tevet does not just recall our grief and mourning for what was destroyed. Like all fasts, it is a call to repent.[16] Jerusalem's fall was ultimately a result of our sins. The Torah speaks of God's overwhelming mercy. Time and again, He sent us prophets, who exhorted us to repent. When they were not obeyed, He had no choice but to allow Nebuchadnezzar, and later on, Titus, to conquer Jerusalem.

The fast of the tenth of Tevet should be more than a torrent of mourning. What sins were committed that caused such widespread death and famine? Why was the punishment so harsh? What can we improve in ourselves? The lessons of the Temple fasts connect us to our past; in Tevet, they should motivate us to work on our own sins, to renew our Jewish souls, to learn more Torah and to do more mitzvot.

EATING BEFORE THE FAST

Fasts generally occur from one evening to the next, or from morning to evening. The Shulchan Aruch briefly discusses whether one can eat in the early morning before fasts from morning to evening,[20] but it does not talk about what foods to eat, except in the case of Tisha B'av. (See Av chapter.) However, here are some helpful tips on the matter:

Do not eat spicy foods, for they induce thirst, and the last thing to do during a fast is think about food, especially since the purpose of a fast is repentance. So to have a clear head, it's best to eat bland or even sweet foods.

(My father always tells us to drink 9 sips of black coffee right before a fast; he says this will prevent thirst the next day. I've been doing this the past few years, and have not usually had a problem with thirst. This could, of course, be coincidence.)

How much should you eat before a fast? Some eat enough for ten people; this is a bit extreme. Eat your fill maybe even a little more than your usual portion but overstuffing is counterproductive, and might even make you sick.

Besides which, eating a large, joyous meal the day before the fast will certainly not put you in the frame of mind for the day ahead.*

Fasting is a matter of control. If you busy yourself with other things but not strenuous exercise, which will make you hungry you won't have time to think about food. Use this time to reflect. Learn something; hear a lecture; take a walk; pray; sleep. There are many activities you can do which have nothing to do with food, and the fast will be over before you know it.

Fasting is more difficult for people who work. If you are one of these people, try to take off at least half a day, to give your body a chance to rest. Those working in Orthodox firms may have an easier time of it.

For Recipes, See Recipe Reference.

---

* except for Yom Kippur, where the last meal before the fast is supposed to be elaborate (See Av chapter).

pass an empty one to his fellow with the other hand."[21]

A Jewish writer, sent to ransom prisoners at the court of Malaga, quotes the king's words upon seeing a re-enactment of this sacrifice: "If this was how the Jews once lived, how can they go on living, now that all this is lost?"[22]

SINS OF OUR FOREFATHERS

According to Midrash Eichah Rabbah, idol worship was the sin most instrumental in our destruction during the First Temple period. As the Midrash says, the ten tribes and the tribes of Benjamin and Judah were likened to two people wearing a new garment during the rainy season. One pulled from one side, and the other pulled from the other, and soon the garment tore. The ten tribes worshipped idols in Shomron, and the two tribes worshipped idols in Jerusalem, until finally they brought about the destruction of Jerusalem.[23]

During the Second Temple period, the cause of the destruction was hatred among our people. This is illustrated by the Talmudic story of Kamtza and Bar Kamtza, where one man's ill treatment of another eventually leads to the Roman conquest of Jerusalem.

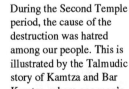

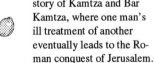

SHEVAT
(JAN. - FEB.)

Torah Counting: Eleventh Month
Regular Counting: Fifth Month

Themes:	The Taste of the Land
	Commitment to Torah
	Israel's Fruits
	Tiberias and Gennosar
	The Tu B'Shevat Seder
	The Seven Species

Foods:	Etrog	Wine

The 7 Species:

Wheat	Barley	Grapes (wine)	Figs
Olives	Dates	Pomegranates	

SHEVAT: THE TASTE OF THE LAND
AND COMMITMENT TO TORAH

The Seven Species

Tu B'Shevat is one of four
new years in the Jewish
calendar. The others are:
The first of Tishrei (for the
judgment of mankind, the
counting of Shmitah, and
the tithing of grain and
vegetables); the first of
Nissan (for counting the

Shevat gives us the chance to taste of the
fruits of Israel, sweet or tart, dripping and juicy
or dried and golden. We savor fruit on Tu
B'Shevat, the New Year for the trees. "Tu"
literally means fifteen; by the fifteenth of the

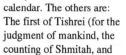

month, most of the winter rains have fallen, and the sap has begun to rise in the trees. The strength of Israel's soil is renewed. Thus, on Tu B'Shevat, we honor the land of Israel by enjoying her fruit, especially the seven species for which the land is praised: wheat, barley, grapes, figs, pomegranates, olives (olive oil) and dates (date honey).[3]

As winter becomes spring, the land is revived. Shevat is an ideal month to reawaken one's spiritual connection to the Torah, as God is renewing the earth's fertility in the land most holy to Him. On the first of Shevat, Moses spoke to the people for the last time before his death, alternately admonishing them for their past sins or strengthening them for their task ahead, in the Promised Land. His farewell address is the entire book of Deuteronomy.[4]

ISRAEL'S FRUIT: "A THOUSAND POINTS OF LIGHT"

Former President Bush might well have been talking about the fruit of the land of Israel when he told of his vision of a "thousand points of light." Every food we eat affects us spiritually. Food can either hamper or heighten our sensitivity to holiness; the Ari (Rabbi Yitzchak Luria) explains that just as the human body extracts vitamins and minerals, the human soul absorbs sparks of holiness that are present in the food. And on Tu B'Shevat, we celebrate God's creation and enhance our spirituality by eating the fruit of the land of Israel, which is filled with these "divine sparks".[6]

reigns of kings and for the three festivals); and the first of Elul (for the tithing of animals).[1]

In the Mishnah, our sages debate the date of the New Year for the trees. Beit Shamai says it's on the first of Shevat, and Beit Hillel says it's on the fifteenth. Today we follow Beit Hillel.[2]

Our ancestors were about to enter the Promised Land, but Moses could not lead the people there because of his sin at the waters of Merivah (Numbers 20:1-13).

DEUTERONOMY: THE "SECOND TORAH"

Deuteronomy is called the "Second Torah" because it repeats many of the episodes already described in the previous books of the Torah. But the stories in Deuteronomy are a form of moral criticism, serving to illustrate the mistakes that were made along the way and prevent their repetition in future journeys.

For instance, we are forbidden to eat beasts of prey, partly because their animalistic tendencies might influence us.[5]

Kabbalists believe that every piece of matter contains divine sparks, stemming from God's spoken words at the moment of Creation.[7]

Apart from Jerusalem, Tiberias is one of the holiest places in Israel. The Talmud attributes the name Tiberias to the Hebrew word *tabur*, which means navel. And Tiberias is the "navel"— the center of the land.[8]

Therefore, the lake in the region is named Kinneret— its fruits are like a *kinor* (harp.)[10]

TIBERIAS: THE JERUSALEM OF FRUITS

As a holiday, Tu B'Shevat has gained in importance since the emergence of Zionism and of the State of Israel.

The fruits in Israel have the most potential for *kedushah* (holiness) in the district of Tiberias. Located in the province of Naphtali, Tiberias gets its holiness from a blessing that Moses bestowed on this tribe (Deuteronomy 33:2-3: "Naphtali is satiated with pleasure and filled with the blessing of Hashem.")

Tiberias is the capital of the Gennosar valley, a lush, fruit-bearing region which exhibits Naphtali's blessing with relish. For the fruits of Gennosar are like a symphony: they tug on the heart and fill the soul with spiritual yearning.[9] The Talmud called Gennosar *Gan Sarim*, the Garden of Princes, for the princes of Israel, our sages, used to visit the valley just to sample its delicious fruits.[11]

FRUIT JAMBOREE

Some people make a special effort to eat a fruit that they have not eaten all year to say a *shehechiyanu* (a blessing over something new). And others eat not just one, or two, but fifteen — count them, fifteen — fruits in honor of the fifteenth of Shevat.[16] Hasidim have a custom of praying on Tu B'Shevat [that next year's etrog will be beautiful.[17]

TU B'SHEVAT: CUSTOMS SHROUDED IN MYSTERY
Wine   Fruits   Etrog

For centuries, Tu B'Shevat was celebrated only with the prohibition of eulogies and community fasts,[12] and the omission of *Tachanun* and *Av Harachamim* from the prayers of the day.[13]

When did the custom to eat fruit on Tu B'Shevat start? The Magen Avraham, an 18th century Torah scholar, mentions it;[14] so does the Mishnah Brurah, a 19th century commentary

on the Shulchan Aruch.[15] But these are late sources, and shed no light on earlier origins.

There is strong historical evidence that the *Ari* (Rabbi Yitzchak Luria), a 15th century Sephardic Kabbalist, observed a Tu B'Shevat Seder. This involved staying up all night on Tu B'Shevat to review texts dealing with different fruits, and, at set intervals, to eat these and other fruits. His disciples continued this practice.[18] These innovative mystics in Sfad saw the act of eating a tree's produce as a way of relating to the miracle of a tree bearing fruit.[19]

The details of that seder were never written down,[21] and, unfortunately, the first written seder we have is in an obscure, highly questionable book called the *Chemdat Hayamim*. Though the author is unknown, the book has been attributed to (among others) Nathan of Gaza, the man who first claimed that Shabbatai Zvi was the Messiah—not a reliable source![22]

This attribution, and some questions about content, caused Ashkenazic[23] authorities to question the validity of the Tu B'Shevat Seder. On the other hand, many Sephardic authorities accept the Seder unquestionably, and many participate in some kind of Seder on this festival.[24]

This version of the Seder uses four cups, like its Passover counterpart; each cup represents a different time of the year. With each cup, we eat a different group of fruits. See the following:

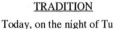

CONTINUING THE TRADITION

Today, on the night of Tu B'Shevat, Sephardic Jews study in their yeshivas all night long. They eat every kind of fruit that can be found in the city. In between the fruits, they pray, sing, and study passages from the Zohar, the Talmud, and the Torah about fruit and trees.[20]

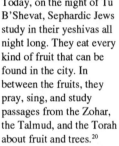

The number of fruits can vary. The Seder which was posted on the Internet had fifteen kinds of fruit. David Geffen's article, "Uncommon Aspects of Tu B'Shvat," listed 20 different fruits to be eaten at the seder.

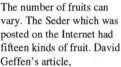
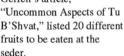

THE FIFTEEN FRUITS

Here they are divided into three categories, representing three different types of people. The first fruits are edible on the inside and inedible outside; it is hard to get to know them, but once you peel away the outside layer, you are rewarded. The second group of fruits are edible on the outside but have an inedible pit. These are the people whom you meet quickly, but never know completely. The third type of fruit is edible both inside and out, like the people who form quick and lasting friendships. As we enjoy all kinds of fruit, so should we know all types of people.

The first of Tishrei, not the fifteenth of Shevat, is the date by which one determines the age of the plant in connection with the law of Orla.

English Translation: Blessed are you, Lord our God, the sovereign of the world, who has created the fruit of the tree.

THE TU B'SHEVAT SEDER[*]
FIRST CUP

Take a cup of white wine, symbolizing the barren winter, and recite the following blessing, with the understanding that this blessing covers all subsequent cups of wine.

Baruch ata Adonai, eloheinu melech haolam, Borei pri hagafen.

(English Translation: Blessed are you, Lord our God, the sovereign of the world, who has created the fruit of the vine.)

Take five fruits from the first group, edible on the inside and inedible on the outside: Pomegranate, almond, tangerine, kiwi, walnut, pistachio, pine nut, chestnut, hazelnut, peanut, grapefruit, coconut, and orange. These symbolize the Kabbalistic world of ACTION (the physical world). Fruits of the seven species are eaten first. Place a fruit that you have not eaten in a year in your right hand.

Now recite the blessings, and have the clear understanding that they cover all the fruit you eat tonight:

Baruch ata Adonai, eloheinu melech haolam, borei pri ha'eitz.

Baruch ata Adonai, eloheinu melech haolam, Shehechiyanu vekeeyamanu vehegeyanu lazman hazeh.

[*] Concisely adapted from the seder at Jerusalem One, compiled by Rivka Zuckerman Matitya and Ilana Sobel.[25]

Now, ask the first question: Why does this holiday honor trees, not events and people?

Judaism has a long tradition of honoring trees: In ancient times, much importance was attached to the first fruits of nature, which were seen as God's gift to mankind. The law of Orla states that one must not eat the fruit of the tree in its first three years. In the fourth year, the fruits were sacred to God, and by the fifth year they could be eaten. Tu B'Shevat is the New Year for the Trees, and so we chose to honor them on this day, when they are judged by God. Many people plant trees in Israel on Tu B'Shevat.[26]

SECOND CUP

The second cup contains 2/3 white wine and 1/3 red wine, symbolizing the onset of Spring. The red is color emerging in the world. Raise the cup in your right hand and drink.

We now take five fruits from the second group, those containing inedible pits which symbolize the Kabbalistic world of Formation: olive, date, peach, persimmon, avocado, apricot, loquat, plum, cherry and mango. Fruits of the seven species are eaten first. Lift up your fruit and enjoy.

Blessed are you, Lord our God, the sovereign of the world, who has kept us alive and sustained us and enabled us to reach this occasion.

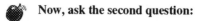

Now, ask the second question:

Why, today, do we specifically eat fruit from the land of Israel?

Tu B'Shevat was the date by which one counted the years for tithing responsibilities in Israel.[27] And as discussed previously, fruit from Israel has spiritual factors that other fruit does not.

THIRD CUP

The third cup is 1/3 white and 2/3 red, for Spring is now progressing. The ground has warmed, and the seeds are taking root and starting to grow. Raise the cup in your right hand and drink up!

We now take five fruits from the third group, those completely edible, representing the Kabbalistic world of Creation: grape, fig, carob, etrog, apple, strawberry, lemon, raspberry, and pear. The Torah may be compared to these fruits, for every part of the Torah is good to study. Again, we first eat fruits of the seven species. Hold the fruit in your right hand and eat.

We us ask the third question: Why do we value conservation?

Honi the circle-maker once saw an old man planting a carob tree. He asked the man, "Why do you plant this tree if you know you will never see its fruits?" The man answered, "I will not see the tree full grown, but my children shall. I plant this tree for my children."

Conservation is a very Jewish concern. The Torah even commands us to let fruit trees stand when we attack a city in wartime. Rabbi Yochanan Ben Zakkai once said, "If you are about to plant a sapling and the Messiah comes, plant the tree and then go to greet the Messiah."

FOURTH CUP

The fourth cup is completely red, for summer has arrived at last. The trees are blossoming and full of fruit. Raise the cup in your right hand and sip.

We do not eat for the fourth cup, as it represents the Kabbalistic world of Emanation, a purely spiritual idea. The world of Emanation is connected with God's love, wisdom and mercy, and His other qualities which are perceived with the heart rather than the senses.

The fourth question: Why are we planting trees when Spring is several months away?

Tu B'Shevat marks the traditional turning point from winter into spring.

THE FRUITS OF THE SEVEN SPECIES
Figs   Dates

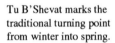

Figs - Sweet, juicy and full of seeds, the fig symbolizes both sin and redemption. Fig leaves were used to cover up Adam and Eve after they sinned with the Tree of Knowledge;[28] some Rabbis claim that the fig was the fruit of the Tree of Knowledge (see Iyar: Apples and the Tree of Knowledge.) So it's not surprising that a fig tree in a dream is a sign that you will preserve your learning.[29] But figs also represent the prosperity of the land; in the days of the Messiah, everyone will sit under his fig and vine[30] tree. And the destruction of Israel is symbolized by a ruined fig tree.[31]

Pomegranates, olives and grapes (wine) were discussed in the chapters of Tishrei, Kislev, and Adar, respectively. Barley and wheat are grains, not fruits.

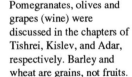

Dates are called *d'vash* (honey) when listed among the seven species. Biblical peoples generally did not have bee honey; instead, they had date or fig honey. And since figs are already listed in the seven species, the honey mentioned must be that of dates.[34]

The date tree is also symbolic of our people, who stand taller than the other nations. And just as date trees never produce less than three fruits, so too we never have less than three righteous men in a generation: like Abraham, Isaac and Jacob, or Hamiah, Mishael and Azariah.[36]

The Talmudic sources on the date are like a single fruit on the branch of a large tree; there are so many that it would take an entire chapter to catalogue them.

THE DATES OF JERICHO

Dates grow well in Jericho; the city is listed four times in the Torah as the "city of dates."[37]

DATES:
FRUIT OF TZIDKUT (RIGHTEOUSNESS)

The sweet, warm taste and wholesome nutrition[32] of the date is like the quality of righteousness. And the Bible and Talmud often make comparisons between the date and righteous men. Deborah the prophetess sat underneath a date palm, passing righteous judgments on the people.[33] In Psalms 92:13, the date tree and the cedar are compared to the righteous man: These trees have no curves, like the righteous; They both have generous shade, and the righteous will thus be rewarded. Their hearts are raised upwards (for they are two of Israel's tallest trees) as the hearts of the righteous are turned towards the heavens. And like the date tree, the righteous person also has desires: desires to follow God.[35]

How apt that dates grow in the land of Israel! For righteousness and Israel are intertwined. Our prosperity in the land is dependent on our good behavior. If we follow God's laws, we are blessed with rain and peace; if we turn away from Him, we are cursed, and ultimately driven out of the land.

So don't complain when your hands are full of date juice on Tu B'Shevat. Instead, be thankful that God has given us a land which will not tolerate sticky fingers!

DATE-NUT BARS

8 ounces dates, finely chopped	1 cup walnuts, chopped medium fine
1 cup raisins	1 orange rind, grated
1 tsp. cinnamon	1 cup sugar

Preheat oven to 350 degrees.

Place dates and walnuts in a medium bowl. Add raisins, grated orange rind, cinnamon, and sugar. Mix in bowl and set aside while preparing batter. This will soften dried fruit.

(From Spice and Spirit, the Lubavitch cookbook.)

OLIVE-ZUCCHINI SALAD

1-2 onions	Salt and pepper to taste
2 cloves garlic	3 tbsp. vinegar
3 tbsp. oil	5 tbsp. tomato sauce
6 medium zucchini	1 tbsp. parsley
3 red peppers	2 tbsp. sugar
1/2 cup olives	paprika

Fry onions and garlic in oil. Add remaining ingredients. Bring to a boil, cover the pot, and cook on a medium flame for 10 minutes.

Serve chilled.

Serves 8.

(Above recipe is from my sister-in-law, Gillian Solomon)

Fruit of the carob tree is a traditional Tu B'Shevat delicacy.

ADAR
(FEB.-MAR.)

Torah Counting: Twelfth Month
Regular Counting: Sixth Month

Themes: Fish: Sign of blessing
          Amalek and Israel
          The Fast of Esther
          Purim: The Purim Feast
          Wine
          Hidden Foods
          Mishloach (Shalach) Manot

Foods: Fish   Wine   Hamantashen
          Kreplach   Vegetables   Mishloach Manot
          Purim Feast Beigli   Sambusak

Our sages suggest that if
one has a court case with a
non-Jew, one should try to
have the case judged in
Adar, the month of our
victory.[2]

ADAR: THE HIDDEN JOY

Rejoice, for the month of Adar is here! Adar
is historically a time of joy and blessing for our
people. In Adar, joy increases, as it decreases in
Av (see chapter on Av).[1] Adar is when we rejoice
over our salvation from the evil decree of
Haman, advisor to King Ahasuerus in the
Persian empire. Haman masterminded a royal
order granting permission to all of Ahasuerus'
subjects (in 127 countries, then most of the

HAMAN AND THE
BLESSING OF ADAR

Haman cast lots, seeking
the best date on which to
destroy the Jews: he
sought a month with no
holidays or fasts by which
we could merit salvation.
Time and time again, the
lot fell on Adar.

known world) to kill our people. With God's help, Mordechai and Esther thwarted this plot and sent out a second decree giving us the power to fight back. So Purim, the fourteenth of Adar, is the celebration of our salvation and of our victory over the forces of Amalek.

ADAR: STRUGGLE BETWEEN AMALEK AND ISRAEL

Amalek has long had a war against the Jews. He was the grandson of Esau, and was raised with an unreasoning hatred of his great-uncle Jacob, which he instilled in his children. He wished only for the chance to destroy Jacob's children. When we escaped from Egypt, Amalek led his people against us, seizing the weaker ones at the back of the line. Until he attacked, the rest of the world was too awed by the miracles of the Exodus to even think of fighting God's chosen people. Many of them were ready to stand with us and with the angels in heaven and praise God with song. But Amalek's attack demonstrated his power which hurt us and diminished the exaltation of God's name that was about to occur. Thus, we have a special commandment to destroy Amalek wherever we may find him.

Today, we are no longer sure who is Amalek, so this commandment is on hold. But in the days of the Messiah, it is said, we will rediscover him, and then the battle will again be joined.

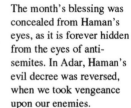

The month's blessing was concealed from Haman's eyes, as it is forever hidden from the eyes of anti-semites. In Adar, Haman's evil decree was reversed, when we took vengeance upon our enemies.

In Shushan and many walled cities, Purim is celebrated on the fifteenth of Adar.

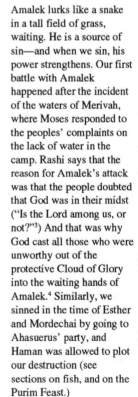

SNAKE IN THE GRASS

Amalek lurks like a snake in a tall field of grass, waiting. He is a source of sin—and when we sin, his power strengthens. Our first battle with Amalek happened after the incident of the waters of Merivah, where Moses responded to the peoples' complaints on the lack of water in the camp. Rashi says that the reason for Amalek's attack was that the people doubted that God was in their midst ("Is the Lord among us, or not?"[3]) And that was why God cast all those who were unworthy out of the protective Cloud of Glory into the waiting hands of Amalek.[4] Similarly, we sinned in the time of Esther and Mordechai by going to Ahasuerus' party, and Haman was allowed to plot our destruction (see sections on fish, and on the Purim Feast.)

Fish did not die during the Flood.

The learned and notable Jews of Shushan fled, determined not to partake of the festival. This is an interpretation of the words "the king made a week-long feast for all the people <u>who were present</u> in Shushan the capitol"— Shouldn't the text have said "all the people"?[5] Therefore, some were not present.

Many commentators point to the words in Esther 9:27, "*kimu v'kiblu*, [the Jews] confirmed and undertook upon themselves," as a hint to this second acceptance of the Torah. The verse speaks about the Jews taking on the holiday of Purim. But the text could

FISH: SIGN OF ADAR, SYMBOL OF BLESSING

Fish   Ahasuerus' feast

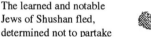

Fish: mysterious symbols of luck that swim in the murky depths of the waters. They are concealed beneath the waves, even from the evil eye, and so they symbolize a blessing that endures. And in Adar, they multiply in the lakes and rivers, a sign of the blessing that is ever-present this month.

But your common flounder are not the only ones blessed in Adar. Israel's sign is rising as well. We are compared to the fish, who live only in the water; we live by the Torah, which is compared to water (See Sivan). And our people and the Torah were elevated twice during this month: when Moses was born (and the Torah was given through him) and in the days of Mordechai and Esther, when we accepted the Torah anew.

During Esther's time, it is said we had sinned so greatly that God proclaimed the destruction of the Jewish community in the form of Haman's decree. Many of our people (not all) attended Ahasuerus' festival, a revelry filled with drinking and licentiousness. Although no one was forced to drink the non-kosher food and wine, they were witness to the desecration of the vessels of the Holy Temple. Ahasuerus profaned these vessels, exhibiting and using them despite their holiness.[6] Our sages note that participation at this event earned us worthy of Haman's decree.[7]

But Mordechai and Esther led the people in repentance, and Haman's evil judgment was repealed. And in Adar, after our second battle with Amalek, we accepted the Torah again. The ultimate blessing of Adar is the peace and joy of returning to God and Torah, and the victory over the evil of Amalek.

simply have said "undertook". The word "confirmed" refers to the fact that we reconfirmed the laws, which we had already undertaken centuries ago,[8] after our first battle with Amalek.[9]

LEMON FISH[10]

1/4 cup salad oil	2 tsp. salt
2 cups sliced onions	1/2 tsp. pepper
6 slices pike, whitefish	2 tomatoes, diced
or salmon	1/2 cup water
2 lemons, sliced thin	2 tsp. sugar
1 tbsp. cider vinegar	1 bay leaf

Heat the oil in a deep skillet. Brown the onions in it. Arrange the fish over the onions and sprinkle with the salt and pepper. Add the tomatoes, lemon slices, water, vinegar, sugar and bay leaf. Cover and cook over low heat 35 minutes. Remove bay leaf. Serve hot or cold.

THE FAST OF ESTHER

On the thirteenth of Adar, we observe the Fast of Esther, abstaining from all food and drink from sunrise until after the Megillah reading that night. Then, our hearts and ears filled with the words of the Book of Esther and the raucous sound of the gragers (noisemakers), we hurry home to break the fast.

Hold onto your hats, people—(especially if they're three-cornered.) The Fast of Esther may be named for our heroine, but despite what people think, it has nothing to do with the three-day fast which she initiated.[11] Esther's fast happened in the middle of Nisan, after Haman issued his famous edict, fully eleven months before the great battle in Adar. And it lasted three days, not one.

Why do we fast on the thirteenth of Adar? To commemorate the fast that we observed on the day of the great battle, when we defended ourselves against the rabid antisemites of Persia; as it was customary to fast before going to war, as a form of prayer and penance. The fast of the thirteenth then has special significance, for it reminds us that God is the one who determines the victors of war, not superior strength or firepower (though those certainly help).

The fast is named for Esther since she initiated the fast of three days the previous Nisan. That fast, and the repentance that she and Mordechai masterminded, were what caused Haman's downfall and Mordechai's rise to power. Therefore, we honor Esther by naming this second fast after her.[12]

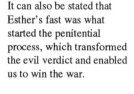

It can also be stated that Esther's fast was what started the penitential process, which transformed the evil verdict and enabled us to win the war.

Maimonides says that the Purim meal must include meat, for it says "days of feasting and gladness (simchah)", and simchah is fulfilled only through meat.[13]

The other three are reading (or hearing) the Megillah, *matanot le'evyonim* (gifts to the poor) and *mishloach (shalach) manot.*

According to Jewish law, most of the meal should be during the day.

THE PURIM FEAST

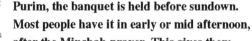

On Purim day we gather with family and friends at a festive table, heaped with meats and wine, to celebrate the *Seudat Purim*, the Purim Banquet. One of four special commandments for Purim, the banquet is held before sundown. Most people have it in early or mid afternoon, after the Minchah prayer. This gives them enough time for a good-sized meal but lets them have the morning and perhaps part of the afternoon to hear the Megillah reading and to deliver shalach-manot.[14]

Purim is a time for partying. Ahasuerus threw one to consolidate his realm, and our sins at that affair put us in dire jeopardy. Esther had two for Ahasuerus and Haman, in order to plead for her people's survival. And when we were safe at last, all of us participated in the first Purim, a day of feasting and celebration, of sending gifts and meals to neighbors and friends (shalach-manot).

That first Purim had a celebratory quality that later Purims lacked. The first rejoicing that follows a reversal is generally more intense than that which comes later.[16]

The Purim Banquet elevates the body and satisfies the soul. In fact, Purim is compared to Yom Kippur, one of the holiest days of the year. On Yom Kippur, we raise ourselves spiritually by afflicting our bodies, but on Purim, we reach the same level of spirituality by pleasuring our bodies. With food and drink, we celebrate the spiritual renewal that we experienced during the time of Mordechai and Esther.[18]

ON TO OUR OWN FEAST!
HIDDEN FOODS AND HIDDEN MIRACLES

Hamantashen   Kreplach
Beigli (or Kindle) Sambusak

"V'anochi Hester Astir Panai—And I will hide my face..."* (Deuteronomy 31:18)

On Purim, we eat foods whose filled centers are hidden by a layer of dough. Sweet, hot

VEGETABLES FOR ESTHER

Some people eat veggies on Purim to remember Esther's courage. She would eat vegetables in the King's palace to avoid eating non-kosher. Good going, Queen Esther![15]

Why did Esther invite Haman to her feasts? Some say that it was to make the King suspicious of Haman.

It is important to give "matanot l'evyonim," (gifts for the poor) on Purim, so that everyone's meal is a cause for celebration.

PURIM AND YOM KIPPURIM: FEASTS AND FASTS

Yom Kippur sounds vaguely like Purim (note the conjunction of that "pur" sound), and indeed, some authorities play on the Yom Kippur's more proper name: *Yom Kipurim*, the Day of Atonement.[17] This word can also be read as *Yom Ki-purim*, a day like Purim, implying that Yom Kippur is only "like" Purim, and of lesser stature.

The real meaning of these names have nothing to do with one another. Purim means "lots," and it refers to the lots that Haman drew to find a day to destroy our people. Yom Kippur is

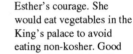

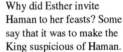

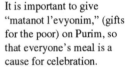

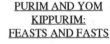
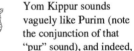

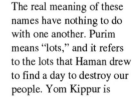

from the root *kaper,* to atone. Yet these holidays are intricately connected. On Purim, we atoned for our sins, and nullified an evil judgment; Yom Kippur is the Day of Atonement. Both holidays have a feast and a fast. On Yom Kippur, the feast precedes the fast, which lasts all day. Purim is a day of feasting, preceded by a fast that commemorates our past atonement.

HAMANTASHEN: BITE OFF HAMAN'S HEAD!

Hamantashen are a mixture of sweet tastes which permeate the tongue in a sensuous way. Add to this the visceral pleasure of doing damage to Haman, of taking a bite of his hat or his ears, and you've got an unbeatable combination. (Some people think that the name comes from the words "*tash Haman,* may Haman's strength weaken".)

But Hamantashen are not just a way of destroying Haman. The original name might have been *muntasche,* pouch of poppy seeds. And the Midrash states that the three corners represent Abraham, Isaac and Jacob, by whose merit we were saved.[20]

hamantashen, often called "*Oznai Haman*" (Haman's ears) or said to represent Haman's hat, are three-cornered pastries filled with prune, poppyseed, or other fruit fillings. Kreplach or meat patties, are hot centers of meat covered in a thin layer of crisply fried dough. The yeast-dough cookies known as *beigli,* resembling little children wrapped in blankets, are eaten by Rumanian Jews. *Sambusak* are usually stuffed with cheese or meat, and eaten by Iraqi, Indian and Persian Jews all year. But on Purim they are filled with dates or chicken.[19]

All of these foods have a center which is hidden by the dough covering, to symbolize the special "hidden" miracles of Purim. The events of the Purim story are not miraculous in the same cosmic sense as the events of Passover. God's hand was clearly visible in the world-shattering, sea-splitting story of the Exodus. In contrast, the heroes of the book of Esther are principally Esther and Mordechai; God's name is not even mentioned. And the book of Esther seems like a series of "lucky breaks." Mordechai just happens to overhear Bigthan and Teresh plotting to kill King Ahasuerus; the king can't sleep, and discovers that he hasn't repaid Mordechai's good deed. At the same time, Haman is lurking at his door. The enormous number of coincidences and the way they come together so perfectly tells us that God was behind the scenes. These events lead to one conclusion: the fall of Haman, and the rise of Mordechai and the Jews of Persia. Purim's miracles are hidden, but their very synchronicity reveals them as miracles.[21]

The hidden foods of Purim symbolize a new age, a time without prophecy, when God concealed His face from us. Even when God's presence was not so overt, His hand was raised, ready to protect His people.

WINE: SANCTIFICATION AND JOY

Drink heartily on Purim... Wine, the symbol of our happiness, was also one of the causes of our salvation. Vashti was killed for refusing Ahasuerus' drunken command to appear naked in his court, and Esther replaced her as Queen; Esther's wine parties brought Haman's downfall. So it's not surprising that our sages require us to drink on Purim until we don't know the difference between "Cursed is Haman" and "Blessed is Mordechai."[22]

Forgetting the difference between Haman and Mordechai would probably take a lot of wine! But our sages did not want us to drink for the sake of having a "good time". While the drinking shows our gratitude and ecstasy at being saved, it also symbolizes something much more spiritual.

Wine on Purim is a sign of our complete faith that God will protect us. Rabbi Eliyahu Ki Tov explains that the lives of our people were always hanging in the balance until the time of Mordechai and Esther. If we committed enough serious sins, we could have been destroyed. Then it happened. Our people earned being destroyed, and would have been,

On Rosh Hashanah and Yom Kippur, kreplach are also traditional, for these holidays also have a hidden aspect which is reflected in the food. (See chapter on Tishrei.)

WINE: SIN AND SANCTITY

Wine has a dual symbolism. It can lead to sin, as it did with Noah, whose son Ham saw him naked in the vineyard (Genesis 9:21-23). Some of our sages claim that the fruit of the Tree of Knowledge was wine. (See section on Tree of Knowledge in Iyar) But wine is also used to sanctify our Sabbath and holidays. The *kiddush* cup is one example of how a substance that can be a source of impurity becomes one of holiness.

THE MERRY DRUNKARD

One drunkard in Cracow carried this idea to extremes. For an entire month two weeks before and after Purim), he would drink even more than usual. This was his reasoning:

Haman was no fool. He knew that it would not be possible to round up all the Jews in one day. So originally, he wanted to

56

order their destruction for a month; during Adar, he would track them down and kill them. But then Haman thought that if his plan failed, the Jews would have an entire month of celebration. This he could not accept, so he limited his edict to a day of execution. So, he reasoned, 'I deem it proper to defeat Haman's plan to limit our enjoyment, and I celebrate the whole month'.[23]

DIVINE MERCY SPEAKS

In the days of Mordechai and Esther, at the time of our repentance, Divine Mercy appeared before the King of Kings. "Oh Lord," said Mercy, "Your sons committed grievous wrongs and gained a harsh decree. They have repented completely with Mordechai and Esther's encouragement. But what if they sin like this again, and do not have such pious and charismatic leaders? Will they then perish?" At that moment, the path of mercy was widened to include all future generations.

but for the efforts of Mordechai and Esther. And their repentance opened a path of divine mercy (see sidebar). They acquired salvation not just for themselves, but for all future generations. The liberal drinking that our sages required of us on Purim carries the implicit statement that we are putting ourselves in God's hands. For even if we, God forbid, lose the ability to tell the difference between right and wrong, God, in his compassion, will protect us from harm.[24]

"CURSED IS HAMAN"/"BLESSED IS MORDECHAI" WHAT DOES IT MEAN?

This is just a sample of what Jewish scholars have said on the matter:

The world is not all Haman, nor is it all Mordechai. There are so many grey areas in between, mixtures of good and evil, that it's possible to lose track of where things are. When you've drunk enough to start blurring these edges, you've fulfilled your obligation.[25]

Mordechai and Haman were both in positions of power. First Haman was on top, and as he fell, Mordechai rose to take his place. This was one of God's mercies, for He could have caused Haman to fall without raising Mordechai. If you can't tell the difference between Haman's rise and Mordechai's, you've fulfilled your obligation.[26]

According to Rabbi Judah Leib Graubart, the famous *Yabia Omer*, these are two time periods. The first was the time of Haman's decree, when our people were sad, suffering with the knowledge that in eleven months they might be exterminated. But as this period was ordained, so too was the time of Mordechai's blessing, when we again rose to prominence. Our sages did not want us to negate the difference between Haman and Mordechai, but to understand that both the plague and the remedy had been ordained by God.[27]

Mishloach (Shalach) Manot

Shalach-manot, the brightly ribboned, boxed, bagged, or otherwise wrapped "care packages," crammed with different foods and goodies, are sent out every Purim to friends and neighbors. Dozens are sent, and dozens arrive at each doorstep, often delivered by children dressed in wild, pretty or bizarre costumes.

The sheer load of shalach-manot that often survives the Purim season can become a burden with Passover only four weeks away, and the house to be cleaned of leaven. In fact, most of what is sent is beyond the minimum necessary to fulfill this (often *very*) filling commandment. You are only required to send two different kinds of foods (meaning foods for which two different blessings are said) to one friend. For it says, *"umishloach manot ish l'rei'eyhu,"* (and the sending of foods each one to his friend).

But those who give only the minimum are missing the whole idea of Purim. This holiday celebrates our brotherhood and unity. The combined efforts of all our people saved us long ago; we celebrate it by giving gifts to the poor (*matanot l'evyonim*) and food to our fellow Jews on Purim day.[30] So the more you give, the better you fulfill the mitzvah.[31]

SHALACH-MANOT: REST FROM WAR

Shalach-manot signify our ancestors' ability to relax after eleven months of tension. For almost a full year, they did not know if they would survive Haman's edict. Once the battle was won, they could sit at their own tables and share their food with friends and neighbors.[28]

These gifts also symbolize the implicit trust they had for one another. At Ahasuerus' party, the food was not kosher and the company was impure, and they committed grave sins. In their own community, they could trust the food and the ethics of their neighbors and friends.[29]

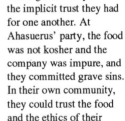

58

We learn this from Nehemiah 8:10, in which Ezra tells the people to eat, drink and be merry on Rosh Hashanah; though it is the day of Judgment, it is a Yom Tov (See Tishrei). The people had been fasting, and there were some who could not prepare the Yom Tov meal in time. So their neighbors sent them manot— food portions, ready to eat, to be used for a meal or exchanged meals with them.

MATANOT
L'EVYONIM-
PARAMOUNT

Our sages put Matanot L'evyonim (gifts to the poor) above the commandments of the Purim Banquet and shaloch manot. According to Maimonides, one should give many gifts to the poor food, money, material objects) and have perhaps a shorter feast or give less shaloch manot. But do not think that gifts to the poor preclude the other commandments.

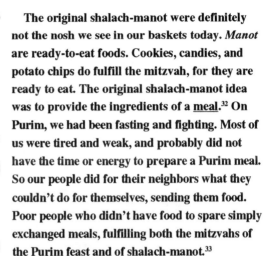

The original shalach-manot were definitely not the nosh we see in our baskets today. *Manot* are ready-to-eat foods. Cookies, candies, and potato chips do fulfill the mitzvah, for they are ready to eat. The original shalach-manot idea was to provide the ingredients of a <u>meal</u>.[32] On Purim, we had been fasting and fighting. Most of us were tired and weak, and probably did not have the time or energy to prepare a Purim meal. So our people did for their neighbors what they couldn't do for themselves, sending them food. Poor people who didn't have food to spare simply exchanged meals, fulfilling both the mitzvahs of the Purim feast and of shalach-manot.[33]

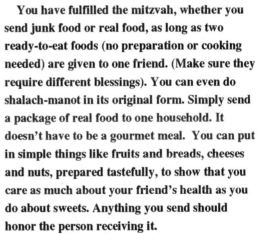

You have fulfilled the mitzvah, whether you send junk food or real food, as long as two ready-to-eat foods (no preparation or cooking needed) are given to one friend. (Make sure they require different blessings). You can even do shalach-manot in its original form. Simply send a package of real food to one household. It doesn't have to be a gourmet meal. You can put in simple things like fruits and breads, cheeses and nuts, prepared tastefully, to show that you care as much about your friend's health as you do about sweets. Anything you send should honor the person receiving it.

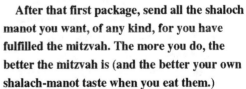

After that first package, send all the shaloch manot you want, of any kind, for you have fulfilled the mitzvah. The more you do, the better the mitzvah is (and the better your own shalach-manot taste when you eat them.)

See Recipe Reference for more Adar recipes.

THE LEAP MONTH
ADAR ALEPH, ADAR BEIT
(FEB.-MAR.)

Torah Counting: Twelfth Month
Regular Counting: Sixth Month

Foods: Mohn (Poppy Seeds)
ARTIFICIALLY CREATED FOODS:
Hydroponics   Soy Foods

TWELVE MONTHS OR THIRTEEN?

Most calendars rarely change. They have the usual twelve months, an extra day every now and then, but that's it. No major shake-ups. And then you have the Jewish calendar, which isn't satisfied with the normal scheme of twelve. Every few years, it adds an extra or "intercalary" <u>month</u> by doubling the month of Adar, creating Adar Aleph (I) and Adar Beit (II), not just twelve months, but thirteen!

The addition of the leap month brought a question of when to observe the delicious holiday of Purim, which would normally occur

Our sages also discuss the question of children born in Adar. Do they celebrate their bar mitzvahs on Adar Aleph or Adar Beit?

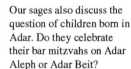

It would be kind of strange to celebrate a holiday only on leap years, wouldn't it?

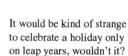

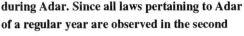

 during Adar. Since all laws pertaining to Adar of a regular year are observed in the second Adar,[1] the first Adar is left pretty bankrupt in terms of foods or holidays. No simmering soups or stews, no succulent food traditions grace the month of Adar Aleph. Since the chapter on Adar already covers all the Purim foods, why bother to write about the leap month at all?

 The leap month is an artificial creation, designed to solve a difficult problem (see section below). It is the perfect time to speak of foods which are not traditional Jewish dishes; foods which were created with human initiative, that have been used to solve some very complex Jewish food problems. Their impact on the Jewish world has gone unnoticed for too long. So be adventurous! This Adar Aleph, come and experience the taste of two foods you might not normally eat.

THE MOON AND THE SUN

The moon, tied to women by their monthly cycles and their celebration of Rosh Hodesh. The sun, ruling the sky during the day, symbol of masculinity. Two polarities with their own, different, values—but they come together in the Jewish calendar.

Did you ever notice that the holidays occur in seasons that echo their spiritual meanings? Adar, the month of our greatest joy, comes when we feel the first ecstasy of spring

WHY CREATE A MONTH?

We inhabit two spheres: the world of the moon and the world of the sun. According to the moon, we set our monthly calendar, the holidays and each New Year (see chapter on Shevat). The sun, however, gives us our seasons; as the earth revolves around that golden light in the sky, we sow our fields and plant our seeds and reap our harvests.

In Jewish tradition, the spheres of the moon and the sun do not exist in a vacuum. Our festivals are determined by the lunar calendar, but they also correspond to the seasons of the

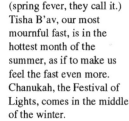

solar year. Don't get me wrong: the only festival which <u>must</u> be observed in a specific season is Passover, which the Torah ties to spring.[2] But once Passover must be celebrated in the spring, the other holidays are, by default, also seasonal. And so, in our tradition, the lunar and solar calendars are joined.

But the sages knew that there was a difference of approximately 11 days between the lunar and solar years. This gap would not matter at first, but within two or three years, our festivals would begin to move back in time. Soon we would be celebrating Passover in the winter, Rosh Hashanah in the summer, and Tisha B'av in the spring! That might make for an easy fast, but all of the seasonal resonances of Passover would be lost.

So we developed a "lunisolar" calendar, adding an extra Adar every few years to keep the months in their proper places. At the end of Shevat, when two witnesses journeyed to Jerusalem to report the sighting of the New Moon, the Sanhedrin (High Court) would decide whether to make that year a leap year.

This system was the epitome of the Torah precept *"lo bashamayim hi,"* literally meaning, "[the Torah] is not in the heavens". The seasons of the festivals are set by Torah law, made in the heavens—but we declare when those festivals occur, by actively sighting the new moon and testifying before the High Court.[3] We are a living part of the chain of Torah and tradition that is passed from generation to generation.

(spring fever, they call it.) Tisha B'av, our most mournful fast, is in the hottest month of the summer, as if to make us feel the fast even more. Chanukah, the Festival of Lights, comes in the middle of the winter.

NONE BUT ADAR!

Why do we double Adar and not Tishrei or Nisan? By Adar, the Sanhedrin (High Court) would know whether spring was coming later or earlier, and thus, whether it was necessary to make that year a leap year.

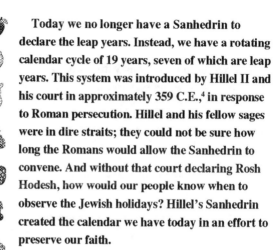

A TIME OF NEED

The Sanhedrin was operating in Teveriah by the time the calendar was instituted, in 359 C.E. For many years, the Jews in Israel had been suffering tremendous persecution at the hands of the Romans.[5] There were attempts at forced conversions; in addition, the Romans tried to prevent us from keeping our laws, especially those that relate to the calendar.[6] Hillel II and his court created the calendar during a brief respite granted by Julianus, the apostate emperor. They did so in the nick of time; the Sanhedrin was forcibly disbanded in 363 C.E., upon the death of Julianus.[7]

The Sanctification of the Moon (Kiddush Levana) that we say today is discussed in the Talmud[8], which was written long before the time of Hillel II. It should not be confused with the Sanhedrin's declaration of the New Moon. (For more information on Kiddush Levana, see Preface.)

A pair arrived from Rakkas.

They had been captured by an eagle

Today we no longer have a Sanhedrin to declare the leap years. Instead, we have a rotating calendar cycle of 19 years, seven of which are leap years. This system was introduced by Hillel II and his court in approximately 359 C.E.,[4] in response to Roman persecution. Hillel and his fellow sages were in dire straits; they could not be sure how long the Romans would allow the Sanhedrin to convene. And without that court declaring Rosh Hodesh, how would our people know when to observe the Jewish holidays? Hillel's Sanhedrin created the calendar we have today in an effort to preserve our faith.

Don't think that we have completely lost the legacy of the Rosh Hodesh declaration! On the Sabbath before Rosh Hodesh, we bless the New Moon, citing the date and time of its first appearance. Although we can not sanctify Rosh Hodesh without a Sanhedrin, we are signalling our commitment to play an active role in the preservation and development of Judaism.

A SECRET CODE

The danger of persecution finally forced the Nasi (head of the Sanhedrin) to communicate with other sages through a secret code. The message below, mentioned in the Talmud[9], was sent by the Nasi to Rava, a sage in Babylonia. The decoded message is brought down by Rashi and the Aruch[10]:

Two scholars sent by the Nasi arrived from Tiberias. They had been captured by the king's officers bearing the eagle (Roman emblem.)

Rashi: They were captured by the Parthians (who controlled Babylonia at the time).

They had been journeying with the ostensible purpose of selling blue cloth.

They were released, and delivered the message, which was the true purpose of their journey.

The Nasi[11] wanted to add an extra month[12] (a leap month).

The Romans would not permit the court to meet.[13]

Nevertheless, the sages of the Sanhedrin[14] convened in Av, and decided to establish a leap month in the following year.[15]

 while carrying articles made in Luz, such as blue cloth (*techailet*).

 Through divine mercy and their own merits, they got away safely.

 The offspring of Nachshon wished to establish a *Nitsiv* (official).

 But the Edomite would not permit it.

 Nevertheless, the masters of gatherings convened and established a Nitsiv in the month in which Aaron the Priest died.

MOHN (POPPY SEEDS)

Mohn, the Yiddish name for poppy seeds, those small black seeds with the tart earthy taste, sounds just like the word moon. The following recipes, appropriately enough, symbolize our reconciliation of the lunar and solar calendar with the addition of Adar Beit:

MOHN COOKIES[16]

3 1/2 cups flour	1 cup vegetable
1/4 tsp. baking soda	shortening
1/2 tsp. baking	1 oz. poppy seed
powder	4 eggs
3/4 cups sugar	1/4 cup water
1/4 tsp. salt	

In large bowl, stir together flour, baking soda, baking powder, sugar and salt. Cut in shortening. Add poppy seed. Break the four eggs into the middle of the bowl, mix with hands. Add water and mix. Roll out to 1/8-inch thickness. Cut into rounds with small glass, dipped in flour so dough won't stick. Bake on greased cookie sheet in 350° oven for 30 minutes until light brown.

MOHN CANDY[17]

| 1/2 cup sugar | 2 cups honey |
| 2 lbs. poppy seeds | 2 cups hazelnuts or almonds halved |

Combine sugar, honey and poppy seeds in a saucepan. Cook over low heat, until thick (30 minutes). Stir often. Add nuts and mix well. Wet a wooden board and pour mixture on it. Pat down until 1/2 inch thick. Cool. Cut with a wet knife into diamond shaped pieces, 2 inches long.

When cool, lift off board. Keep indefinitely.

HYDROPONICS: CREATING
NEW FOOD SOURCES

Soil is as soil does—that's what Knopf and Zax, 19th century researchers, were saying when they came up with the idea for hydroponics. If you can find something that gives the support and nutrients of soil, then you can grow plants without it. Knopf and Zax probably never anticipated how their idea would be developed, and what a blessing it would be for Israel.[18]

Hydroponics was first used as a farming method in the Pacific Islands and Japan, and has since spread to many countries around the world, including the United States and Israel.[19] Three substitutes for soil have been developed: water, gravel, and sand. The hydroponics farmer adds balanced solutions of chemicals and nutrients, and monitors the light and heat of the plants as they grow. The process can be, and must be, perfectly controlled, one of hydroponics' biggest advantages. Problems with acidity, root disease, lack of water? These can be things of the past with hydroponics.

In 1936, Z. Soskin was the first to experiment with hydroponics in Israel. Since then, Israel has been one of the most advanced countries in terms of hydroponics research. Hydroponics operations in Israel have utilized water, sand, mica and peat solutions, among many others. Now a Jewish Agency laboratory in Be'er Sheva is experimenting with salt-water solutions. These experiments have served Israel well; hydroponically grown vegetables have been a boon in areas with little or no farming soil (like the Negev). Wondrous, to be able to grow food in communities without soil!

Hydroponics has (literally) proven a Godsend for religious farms in Israel. According to Jewish law, we are not allowed to work the land of Israel during Shmitah year, the last year of a continuous seven-year cycle. Jews living in Israel have had to rely on food sold by non-Jews or food brought in from overseas. Hydroponics gave these farmers a new source of food. For, the Torah says "*Shabtah Ha'aretz-* And the Land shall rest"... but it says nothing about nutrient-saturated sand solutions.

The day when hydroponics is a solution to world hunger is still far off. There are too many problems, both technical and economic, to launch a large commercial enterprise. But this farming method is a symbol of the creative power and possibilities of which we, as a people, are capable. Let us hope that the experiments underway in Israel further expand the role of this unique method of farming.[20]

SOY FOODS: WIDENING THE JEWISH PALATE

When is a cheeseburger not a cheeseburger? When it's made with soy cheese, of course!

Soy foods make the kosher taste experience just a little broader. The range of kosher soy products includes: pareve ice creams such as Tofutti; soy milk for the lactose intolerant and soy formulas, such as Isomil, for babies; and soy cheeses and meats, part of a larger industry of kosher substitutes for bacon, shrimp and other foods.

Soy also brings health benefits. Studies have shown that soybeans and soy products decrease the risk of colon and rectal cancer; researchers speculate that the little noted soybean inhibits the transformation of normal cells into cancer cells. Other studies have linked soybeans to reduced breast cancer risk. Soybeans are full of isoflavins, which may keep estrogen from binding to cells and forming tumors.[21]

So bite into that soy—it's healthy for you, and kosher too!

NISAN
(MAR.-APRIL)

Torah Counting: First Month
Regular Counting: Seventh Month

Themes: Month of Freedom
         Rosh Chodoshim
         The Harvest and Omer
         Chametz and Matzah
         The Seder Plate
         The women of Passover
         Miriam the Prophetess

Foods:	Matzah	Maror	Charoset	Chazeret
Lamb	Wheat	Oats	Barley	
Spelt (Primitive Grain)			Rye	Walnuts
Apples	Romaine Lettuce	Horseradish		
Miriam's Well				

Nisan: Month of Freedom

On the fifteenth of Nisan, our people forever left Egypt, the land of their slavery. We were redeemed from the servitude of mortar and bricks, building the cities of Pitom and Ramses (Exodus 1:11) Our foremothers knew that no longer would their sons be used as bricks in the pyramids; no longer would they be thrown into

NISAN: FIRST MONTH OF SPRING

Nisan is *Chodesh Ha'aviv*, the month of Spring; now seeds begin to sprout and flowers start to grow. Even the word *Nisan* (which is Babylonian in origin) bears a strange resemblance to the Hebrew word *nitzan* or bud.

Blossoms are so prevalent in Nisan that the blessing said on trees in flower is especially applicable during this month. Some authorities rule that this blessing should only be said in Nisan.[1]

the Nile (Exodus 1:22). God had heard our suffering; we saw with our own eyes the ten plagues that He inflicted on Egypt, and the killing of the Egyptians' first-born sons. And in Nisan we saw the greatest of miracles: the dividing of the Red Sea and the drowning of the Egyptian army that pursued us.

Nisan contains all the joy that we felt at this magnificent moment. At this miracle Moses sang a song of praise for God; Miriam the Prophetess took her timbrel and led the women in dance and song, so ecstatic and hopeful was she about the future of her people (Exodus 15:1-21). Nisan, the month of redemption and miracles, is filled with this exhilaration. Throughout it, we do not fast, eulogize the dead, or recite Tachanun.[3] And on the fifteenth of Nisan, we observe the holiday of Passover, commemorating our deliverance from Egyptian bondage after generations of slavery.

The Exodus was so important that Nisan is called *Rosh Chodoshim* or the head of all the months (Exodus 12:2). At the New Moon, God commanded Moses and Aaron to count Nisan as the first month of the year. Since the Torah never names the months, but instead numbers them, every mention of a date reminds us of the Exodus[5]. And it is a greater mitzvah to sanctify Nisan than it is to sanctify any other month.[6]

The themes of redemption and freedom, of kingship and slavery, are present in our Passover food. Our ancestors worked hard providing bricks for cruel, foreign kings. Like them, we spend our strength doing backbreaking work:

PARSHAT HACHODESH

We read *Parshat Hachodesh*, the passage which describes the primacy of Nisan (Exodus 12:2) on the Shabbat before, or the Shabbat of Rosh Chodesh Nisan. This gives the month greater honor and reminds us that Passover, the first of the three festivals, is approaching.[2]

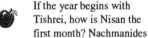

FIRST IT SHALL BE

If the year begins with Tishrei, how is Nisan the first month? Nachmanides says it is first for redemption;[4] Eliyahu Ki Tov says that Nisan has more potential for miracles and new things than any other month. The Hebrew word for year (*shanah*) sounds like the word for old (*yashan*). Most of the world have only a fixed year, a *shanah*. But God gave us, His people, something more. In Nisan, we have the concept of *Rosh Chodoshim*, the head of the months; the word *chodesh* (month), with a simple change of vowels, becomes *chadash* (new). So the Torah says, "First shall it be to you": the first in miracles, and only to you.[7]

Is there enough room in the year for two first months? Not according to some authorities. They hold that one can only refer to secular months by <u>name</u> on official documents, or one would break the commandment: "The first shall it be to you of the months of the year."[8]

We are traditionally a pastoral people. Jacob worked as a shepherd for Laban for fourteen years; Moses took care of Jethro's sheep. Hence, many of our holidays and months have an added, agricultural focus.

The harvest is a long process. Crops are planted in the Spring; they grow until Shavuot, when they are cut and left standing in the field to dry. During Tishrei, the crop is gathered in from the fields. (That's why Shavuot is called *Chag Hakatzir* (The Holiday of the Harvest), and Succot is called *Chag Ha'asif* (The Holiday of the Gathering.)

Barley is the first grain to grow during the harvest season. And it is cut for the Omer offering on the sixteenth, even though it is a Yom Tov and harvesting is forbidden, for the commandment is specific for that day.[12]

searching out and destroying any bit of Chametz, or leaven in our possession. But unlike them, we are working on our own for a greater master, for the king of kings himself. When we are done, we lean back in our chairs and enjoy the fruits of our labor, noshing soups, chicken and matzah kugel at the Seder meal.

THE HARVEST AND THE OMER
Barley   Wheat

By Passover, the harvest is already approaching and our crops are being judged for the coming year. But the rain that we prayed for in the winter[9] would now be a curse, for the Spring crops are already starting to grow, and rain would spoil them. So on the second day of Passover (the sixteenth of Nisan), we pray instead for dew. And in the Shemonah Esrai, we stop saying *Mashiv Haruach Umorid Hagashem* (Who causes the wind to blow and the rain to fall) and say instead *Morid Hatal* (Who brings down the dew.) And on Passover, our crops are judged for the coming year.[10]

The Omer offering was brought to the Temple, also on the sixteenth of Nisan. On the night of the sixteenth, a sheaf of barley is cut. That morning, it is brought as a meal offering with the usual Musaf sacrifice.[11] This bit of barley is not just a simple sacrifice; the Omer offering is the cutoff point between *yashan* (old grain) and *chadash* (new grain). Yashan can be used right away, but chadash must wait until the next Omer offering (when it becomes yashan). That is why matzahs for Passover are made from wheat grown in the previous winter's harvest![13]

CHAMETZ AND MATZAH

Water

Flour: **Wheat** **Barley** **Oats** **Rye**
Spelt (Primitive Grain)

Most people think of chametz or leaven as a rich, soft loaf of white bread fresh from the oven. Or as a hot, crumbling, buttery breakfast muffin. Or even as a simple tea biscuit. But few realize that leaven can also be a sheaf or stalk from the five species of grain (wheat, barley, oats, rye, or spelt) standing in the field, wet and fermented. Most of these foods sound heavenly, but eating them on Passover will not get you to heaven at all. Far from it! Eating anything that comes under the heading of "Chametz" merits one of the strictest punishments in Jewish law: the dreaded *Kareit*, or a loss of one's soul by way of the heavenly court. (This was prevented by giving the sinner *malkut*, a private lashing).[14]

And then there's matzah. This flat, crumbly "non-bread," like the "rich" chametzdik breads, can also only be made from the five species of grain. But matzah, with its crisp, charcoal taste, is called *Lechem oni*, the bread of affliction, because it was fed to our ancestors in Egypt. And on the eve of the Exodus, when they were too rushed to wait for the bread to rise, they baked it as food for their journey. On Passover, the holiday of freedom, we must eat only matzah, which reminds us of our former state of slavery.

And then there are prohibitions against benefiting from Chametz or seeing it in your possession.

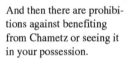

MATZAH: A HARD BREAD TO BAKE

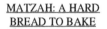

To bake matzah, you need the vigilance of a detective. From the moment it is milled (and in the case of Shmurah matzah, from the time it is harvested), the grain is put under strict surveillance. The criminal, in this case, is not the wheat itself but one of the more common elements, a culprit found in the very air we breathe: water. For H_2O, and most liquids, cause the wheat to ferment, making it chametz. (Gives new meaning to the phrase "water contamination").

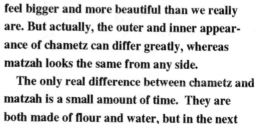

So we guard the grain, and then the flour, with eagle eyes. And with equal vigilance, we watch the baking matzah to be sure that it is in the oven for less than eighteen minutes. Any more than that, and the dough would start to rise, and the matzah would become one of Passover's most forbidden foods: chametz.[16]

The water used in baking the matzah must sit for twelve hours to insure that it stays cool in temperature.[17]

Egypt was a society founded on pride. The stronger preyed on the weaker; there was no nation not subject to Egypt at the time of the Exodus. Pharoah's proclamation, "Who is God that I should listen to Him" is but an echo of the general Egyptian attitude.[19]

We strive to be humble like matzah. And even during their darkest hours in Egypt, our ancestors treated each other kindly. For one who has been poor can identify more easily with the suffering of others.[20]

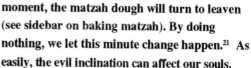

This might be seen as a contradiction. Why, if we are celebrating our liberation from slavery, do we deny ourselves the wide array of leavened breads and cakes which are available to us?

This question confuses liberation and license. We didn't escape from Egypt on our own; God took us out with a strong hand.[15] And once free of the tyrannical Eygptian slave masters, are we to ignore the One who saved us, who made a covenant with our forefathers and kept it?

So we go on a search—and destroy—mission, looking carefully through our homes for any trace of chametz. And this has yet a secondary symbolism. For leaven, which is puffed up and filled with hot air, is the arrogance that leads us to sin. Matzah, however, is completely flat; it represents humility. It signifies the realization that we are not perfect beings, and that God stands above us all. So as we eradicate the offending crumbs, we are also seeking to rid our souls of any trace of pride or sin.[18]

Like the evil inclination, leaven is deceptive. It is more beautiful than matzah, and has a more pleasant taste. And the evil inclination makes us feel bigger and more beautiful than we really are. But actually, the outer and inner appearance of chametz can differ greatly, whereas matzah looks the same from any side.

The only real difference between chametz and matzah is a small amount of time. They are both made of flour and water, but in the next moment, the matzah dough will turn to leaven (see sidebar on baking matzah). By doing nothing, we let this minute change happen.[21] As easily, the evil inclination can affect our souls.

THE PASSOVER LAMB
Lamb   Roasted meat

In Egypt, on the fourteenth of Nisan, the sound of bleating and the smell of fresh blood filled the air. This was not another plague, but a scene of worship. In every Jewish house, the lamb, an Egyptian god, was being slaughtered for the Passover sacrifice.

By the next night, the smell of slaughter had been replaced by another scent: the smoky, hot aroma of roasting lamb, tender, juicy and delicious. And Jewish families sat together, talking and laughing, eating their Passover lamb, while their Egyptian neighbors wailed over the death of their first born. For the Angel of Death saw the lambs' blood that our forefathers had smeared on their doorposts, and passed them over.

Every year after the Exodus, the Passover lamb was sacrificed. And today we remember the sacrifice by setting a broiled shankbone, usually from chicken, on the Seder plate. But this piece of meat is just for show; Jews are not allowed to eat anything roasted on the Seder nights of Passover. So put those Spring Lamb dishes on the backburner. There'll be time for them later.[24]

WHY THE LAMB?

It took a lot of courage to sacrifice a lamb in Egypt. While they are plentiful in the Spring, and easy to get, lambs were also worshipped by the Egyptians. The lambs were gathered and tethered on the tenth, in full view of the

The similarity between chametz and matzah is reflected in the Hebrew. They share the same letters, with one exception. Matzah ends in a "hey" ( ) and chametz begins in a "chet." ( ) The difference between the letters is one small line.[22]

HEARTY APPETITE!

The laws of eating the Passover lamb are complex, to say the least. Just a taste: The lamb was completely roasted, not cooked, and it was eaten at night on the fifteenth, the day after it was sacrificed. Matzahs and maror (bitter herbs) were eaten at the same time. No leftovers for this meal: all parts of the lamb were either burned or eaten. It wasn't hard to eat all that meat- families were allowed to eat together and share one lamb![23]

During the Seder, some Haggadahs will mistakenly tell you to raise the shankbone, or point to it, when we mention the Passover sacrifice. This is a Halachic problem. For sacrifices are no longer permitted, and we don't want people to think that we actually slaughtered the animal for the Passover sacrifice.[25]

Egyptians. And when the Egyptians asked us what we were doing, we didn't hide our plans. So during the month whose zodiacal sign is the ram, our ancestors had faith that God would give them protection. And the Pesach lamb was a sign that God was more powerful than either the god or the might of the Egyptians.

That the Egyptians didn't take revenge was one of God's many miracles.

THE SEDER PLATE

Egg	Potatoes	Celery
Bitter Herbs	Horseradish	Endives
Shankbone	Romaine Lettuce	Charoset
Salt Water	Wine	

Two other orders for the Seder plate:

Beytzah   Zeroa
Charoses   Maror
    3 Matzahs
Salt
Water   Karpas

(Rabbi Moshe Iserlis)

Charoses   Maror
    2 Matzahs
Beytzah   Zeroa

(The Vilna Gaon)[27]

Beytzah (Egg)   *Zeroa*
        Maror (Bitter Herbs)
Karpas   *Charoses*
        Chazeret

The Seder plate above is what most people see on Seder tables. The arrangement is by the Ari (Rabbi Isaac of Luria), a sixteenth century Spanish kabbalist.[26]

Beytzah or egg reminds us of the Chagigah (Festival) sacrifice, a peace offering which was brought with the Passover lamb. The egg on the Seder plate is a sign that we mourn the loss of our Temple sacrifices. And at the same time, it reminds us that Spring is here.

Many kinds of kosher animal were brought for the Chagigah sacrifice: sheep or cattle, large or small, male or female.

Eggs are a symbol of fertility, but they also represent mourning. (See section on Tisha B'Av.) Their round shapes are like the "wheel of life" which is always turning. And eggs have no openings, so they remind us tnot to complain about our ultimate fate.[30]

But the egg goes beyond the Seder plate; Ashkenazi Jews customarily eat eggs (often dipped in salt water) during the Seder meal. For the egg, which hardens when boiled, is like our people, who become stronger with persecution.[28]

The egg has no openings; we pray that the mouths of our enemies, like the egg, will remain shut[29] And as the egg is sealed in its casing, so should we be protected from those who seek to destroy us.

This custom originated as a rejection of ancient pagan customs, for the ancient Egyptians would not eat the by-products of the animals they worshipped.[31]

Zeroa, the shankbone, serves as a reminder of the Passover lamb (see section above.)

Maror (Bitter Herbs)—We echo the tears of our ancestors in Egypt as we grate the bitter herbs (usually a horseradish) for the Seder. And the bitter taste of this dish is a reminder of our slavery in Egypt. Maror is eaten twice at the Seder meal, first alone and then with matzah (and sometimes charoses) for *Korech* (a part of the seder.)

Chazeret—The core of a romaine lettuce. Many eat this vegetable in place of the horseradish maror.

Karpas—Who can forget steaming, boiled potatoes dipped in <u>real</u> salt water? (The kind where you can taste the salt on the tip of your tongue...) The vegetable can be anything that's not bitter, eaten in its normal fashion (raw or cooked.) These greens, dipped in salt water, are a strange combination of pain and pleasure. The dipping is a sign of ease and luxury and alludes to the fact that on this night, we are considered kings. Yet the salt water is a reminder of the tears our people shed as Egyptian slaves.

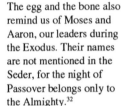
The egg and the bone also remind us of Moses and Aaron, our leaders during the Exodus. Their names are not mentioned in the Seder, for the night of Passover belongs only to the Almighty.[32]

It's hard to eat the required amount of Maror if one uses horseradish. So some people use romaine lettuce instead, which has a bitter taste if left in the ground long enough. (If you use romaine lettuce, be careful to wash out all those bugs!) And others use endives as a substitute.[33]

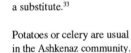
Potatoes or celery are usual in the Ashkenaz community.

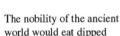
The nobility of the ancient world would eat dipped foods as an appetizer.

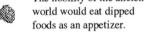

This dual symbolism is typical of Passover, which often juxtaposes two opposing concepts in the same ceremony.

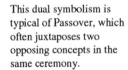

74

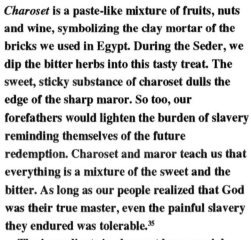

Recipes for charoset vary according to your city of origin: A major Ashkenazi recipe utilizes apples, walnuts, almonds, cinnamon, wine and ginger. Sephardim may add raisins, dates, figs, oranges, coriander and chili pepper.[34]

Charoset is a paste-like mixture of fruits, nuts and wine, symbolizing the clay mortar of the bricks we used in Egypt. During the Seder, we dip the bitter herbs into this tasty treat. The sweet, sticky substance of charoset dulls the edge of the sharp maror. So too, our forefathers would lighten the burden of slavery reminding themselves of the future redemption. Charoset and maror teach us that everything is a mixture of the sweet and the bitter. As long as our people realized that God was their true master, even the painful slavery they endured was tolerable.[35]

The ingredients in charoset have special significance. Some have been used to describe our people. In Song of Solomon, we are compared to figs, dates, nuts, apples, and pomegranates. Others relate to the pain and suffering we endured in Egypt. Cinnamon and ginger, the spices used in charoset, are sometimes not finely grated, so that bits and pieces stick out in the mixture like the straw that we used in our labor. Charoset wine is generally red, like the Jewish blood that was spilled in Egypt: the blood of the Jewish babies in which Pharoah would bathe; the blood from the lashes of our overseers; the blood of the innocent babies thrown heedlessly into the Nile.[36] In addition, it recalls the blood of the Passover sacrifice.

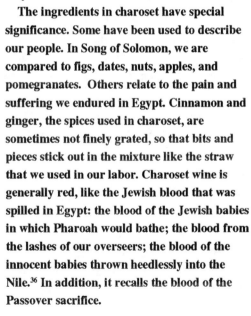

Apple trees symbolize our modesty and faith. For in Egypt, Jewish women would conceal their pains and give birth in the fields, under the apple tree. Why the apple tree? Because they knew that the leaves of the apple tree only appear after the fruit, to protect it. Thus, they would give birth, and God would protect them.[37]

These charoset recipes taken from Girl's Town/Or Chodosh complimentary card:

CHAROSET- ASHKENAZ

1 lb. apples
1 1/4 cups walnut halves
3/4 tbsp. ground cinnamon
3 to 5 tbsp. sweet wine
a dash of ginger

Peel, core, and chop the apples. Add the walnuts and chop finely.

Add the cinnamon, wine and ginger and mix well. The charoset should have the texture of a coarse paste. Taste and add more cinnamon or wine.

CHAROSET- SEPHARAD

1 cup pitted dates (about 1/2 lb.)	1/2 cup raisins
1 apple	1/2 cup walnut pieces
1 tsp. grated fresh ginger	1/4 sweet wine

Combine all the ingredients except the wine in a wooden bowl and chop finely. Stir in the wine to make a coarse paste.

WHAT TO DO WITH YOUR LEFTOVER CHAROSET[38]

8 large apples
6 oz. sweet wine

Core the apples. If it is your custom to eat only those fruits that are peeled, you may do so.

Fill the center of the apple with charoset leftover from the Seder. Place the apples in a baking pan and pour the wine over them. Cover with foil. The apples should be close, but not touching.

Bake at 375 degrees for 15-20 minutes. Remove the foil and continue to bake until they are soft enough so that your fork can spear them, but not squashy.

Serve hot or cold.

THE FOUR CUPS OF WINE

Are all cups of wine equal? Not on Passover, when we must drink four cups of wine, and only four cups, each in their proper place in the Haggadah ceremony. Only then do we fullfill the commandment of telling the story of the Exodus.[39]

But the wine is also symbolic of the Exodus itself; each cup represents a phase of the story in Egypt. In fact, according to our sages in the Jerusalem Talmud, the cups symbolize the four stages of redemption. These are: *Vehotzaiti*— "I bring you out from the burdens of Egypt"; *Vehitzalti*— "I will deliver you from slavery"; *Vega'alti*— "I will redeem you with an outstretched hand"; *Velakachti*— "I will take you unto me for a people and I will be your God." The flowing wine is a sign of our joy that God has fulfilled His promises, and that He will do so in the future. The bubbling fluid is like God's power, erupting against our enemies. Our ancestors sang and danced after crossing the Red Sea. May we have cause to rejoice soon, with the coming of the Messiah and the third redemption.

WOMEN AND PASSOVER

The midwives
The women of Egypt
Miriam the Prophetess
Miriam's Well

As with Chanukah, women figure greatly in the Passover miracle. Let us journey to ancient

Are women obligated in the four cups? They would not have been, because by Jewish law, women are exempt from all positive time-bound commandments.[40] But women had a major part in the Exodus (see section on Women and Passover), so they, too, must drink up![41]

The four cups also refer to Babylon, Persia, Greece, and Rome, the four kingdoms which subjugated Israel after the Exodus. And God will mete out four types of punishment for the suffering they caused us.[42]

Egypt and learn of the strength and *mesirut nefesh* (self-sacrifice) of our sisters, whose devotion to God and to their own people was our salvation.

THE MIDWIVES

In Exodus 1:15-20, we are told that Pharoah, determined to eradicate the Hebrew people, instructed the Hebrews' midwives to kill their male children and let all the women live. Yet these two heroines, named by the Torah as Shifrah and Puah, feared God more than the king. They resisted Pharoah's decree, allowing all the Jewish babies to live. And when Pharoah called his rebellious servants to the carpet, they claimed that it was the fault of the Hebrew women, who always gave birth before the midwives visited them. Pharoah saw that the midwives would not cooperate, so he openly commanded his people to throw Jewish male newborns into the Nile.

The Torah doesn't tell us much about these courageous woman. It gives us names but no lineage. And because they are called "Meyaldot Haivriot," which can mean either Hebrew midwives or midwives for the Hebrews, we are not even sure if they're Jewish or Egyptian.

This scriptural ambiguity has produced two parallel traditions, explained by Nehama Leibowitz, scholar of <u>*Studies in Exodus.*</u>[45] The first opinion is that the midwives were Jewish. In the Babylonian Talmud, tractate Sotah 11b, Rav and Shmuel argue over whether the

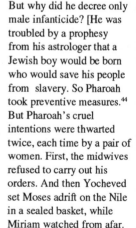

AND PHAROAH SAID: "KILL THE MALES!"

The story of the midwives shows Pharoah's sly strategy of gradual oppression of our people. He couldn't openly kill us, for it would have seemed cruel to wantonly murder a people who had been invited into the land by his predecessor. So he began by imposing a labor tax, and he secretly ordered the midwives to kill all Jewish newborn males.[43]

But why did he decree only male infanticide? [He was troubled by a prophesy from his astrologer that a Jewish boy would be born who would save his people from slavery. So Pharoah took preventive measures.[44] But Pharoah's cruel intentions were thwarted twice, each time by a pair of women. First, the midwives refused to carry out his orders. And then Yocheved set Moses adrift on the Nile in a sealed basket, while Miriam watched from afar.

WHY "SHIFRA" AND "PUAH"?

Rashi explains that Yocheved was called Shifra because she would make the children beautiful (meshaperet) and Miriam was called Puah because she knew how to calm the babies down by purring (po'ah) and cooing at them.[46] (For more on Miriam, see the section on Miriam's well.)

ONLY TWO?

And how were there only two midwives for all of the Hebrew women? Several commentaries explain that there were actually 500 midwives; Shifra and Puah were simply the head midwives, who were responsible for collecting taxes for Pharoah from the others. Pharoah was simply giving his orders through Shifrah and Puah.[47]

midwives were Yocheved (Moses' mother) and Miriam (Moses' sister) or Yocheved and Elisheva (Aaron's wife). Rashi, Ibn Ezra, Nachmanides, and Rashbam also bring this opinion in their commentaries. The second opinion, cited by Josephus, Midrash Tadsheh, the commentary Imrei No'am, and Shadal, states that the midwives were righteous Egyptians.

The midwives were Egyptians? Shocking. And yet, this is more logical in context. Would Pharoah have commanded Jewish midwives to kill their own people if he wanted to keep his plan secret? And as several commentaries point out, this would explain why the Torah tells us that Shifrah and Puah feared God more than Pharoah. If they are Jews, it wouldn't be so surprising. But if they are gentiles, then this is praise indeed!

But I find it hard to give up the idea that the midwives were Jewish, and especially that they were Miriam and Yocheved. Besides the opinions of Rashi, Nachmanides, Rashbam, and Ibn Ezra, which should not be taken lightly, I have found several midrashim in Exodus Rabbah I which mention Miriam and Yocheved, or Yocheved and Elisheva, as midwives. There must be a very old tradition working here; and doesn't it make you far prouder to think that two of Judaism's greatest heroines stood up against Pharoah?

THE JEWISH WIVES IN EGYPT

The midrash says: Our ancestors were saved in Egypt to the merit of righteous women. For they kept our people alive; when the men were exhausted from their work, the women would feed them and bathe them and tend to them. And they took down their brass mirrors and made themselves up in their prettiest dresses, scented oils and make-up, so that their husbands would desire them in spite of their fatigue.[49]

Pharoah was determined to stop us from multiplying. He commanded his overseers to decree that the men could not go home to their wives, but must sleep in the fields at night. "After all," said the overseers to the Jews, "by the time you go home and come back, it will already be noon, and how will you complete your quota for the day?" But God helped the wise women of Israel; when they drew water from their wells that day, fish were plentiful there. Then the women went to their men in the fields, and washed and fed them. And then they slept side by side in the hidden places of the fields.[51]

MIRIAM THE PROPHETESS
AND THE TENTH OF NISAN

On the tenth of Nisan, after forty years in the desert, Miriam was taken peacefully by God. While she had never had the same public role that her brothers Moses and Aaron did, she was a prophetess in her own right, and a leader of the people in Egypt. Miriam was one of our

The midrash notes that the women were rewarded for their valor when Bezalel built the Tabernacle. At that time, Moses asked the people for gifts, and the women brought forth their brass mirrors. Moses did not know whether to accept their contribution; God told him to take the mirrors because they had been used for a holy purpose. Fittingly, the mirrors became the *kiyor*, the basin in which the Priests washed their hands for purification.[48]

The Talmud relates that the Jewish men had divorced their wives because they despaired of having children who would be thrown in the Nile.[50]

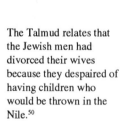

Miriam prophesied even before Moses; when he was but a fetus, she said that her mother would have a boy who would become the savior of Israel. And when they had to put the baby into the Nile, Miriam kept watch over her brother to see what would become of her prophecy.[52]

Some authorities say that Miriam and Yocheved were the midwives (see previous section on the midwives.)

The other two benefactors were Moses and Aaron. Moses' merit brought us the manna, and Aaron's gave us the clouds of glory, which sheltered us from the elements.[53]

three benefactors in the desert; Her righteousness won us what became known as Miriam's well— a sieve-like rock which gushed water and traveled with our people in the desert. Therefore, some people fast on the tenth of Nisan in remembrance of Miriam.

SOME FACTS ABOUT MIRIAM'S WELL

This well, a spring of healing, traveled with our people as they moved through the desert, settling opposite the Tabernacle every time they made camp. It would form rivers which separated between family and tribe, so that all knew their place in the camp (Yalkut Pikudey). It has not disappeared; One can supposedly see it, now a sieve-like rock in the sea, from the top of Mount Carmel (Shabbat 35). There is a custom to draw water at the end of the Shabbos, for Miriam's well fills all other wells at this time (Kol Bo).[54]

For other Nisan recipes, see Recipe Reference.

Gathering the Manna
(painting by Poussin, 1841 France)

IYAR
(APRIL-MAY)

Torah Counting: Month Two
Regular counting: Eighth Month

Themes: Manna
          Quail
          Pesach Sheini
          Lag B'omer
          The Controversy Over Meron

Foods:	Manna	Tamarisk Tree Sap	Coriander
	Challah	Quail	Matzoh
	Cooked Eggs	Campfires	

Food in Iyar

The splendor of the month of Iyar (called *Chodesh Ziv,* or the month of Glory) is present in the tasty range of foods, both natural and miraculous, which blossom at this time. The harvest season, which began last month, is coming to fruition now. The tender shoots which start appearing at this time are signs of God's power on earth and the physical rejuvenation of the world after winter.[1]

Moses told the Israelites to bring pure olive oil, beaten for the menorah, to be an Eternal light.

Exodus 27

When did the Manna Fall?

The Biblical account is vague on dates. In Exodus 16:1, the Torah notes that the Jews entered the Sinai desert on the fifteenth of Iyar. This is the only date mentioned. Soon after, our people complained to Moses and Aaron. In response, God told Moses (Exodus 16:4): "Behold I will cause to rain for you bread from the heaven." By the next morning, the manna had fallen. Rashi says that the manna fell on the sixteenth of Iyar, the morning after the Jews entered the desert.[5] The Chatam Sofer, a 19th century scholar, connects the fall of the manna to the holiday of Lag B'omer (see Lag B'omer), which takes place on the 18th of Iyar.[7]

By Shavuot (the sixth of Sivan), we bring the first fruits which we have gathered to Jerusalem as a gift of thanksgiving.

During Iyar, God granted us the miracle of manna, a tasty bread which fell from the sky and sustained our people in the desert for forty years. Not once did we become ill from the manna, the "bread of the strong (*lechem abirim*)," which was completely digested, leaving no waste products. Thus, Iyar is also a month of healing,[2] and plants and foods of healing are especially pertinent. First, we tell about manna: how it fell, what it was, and what it meant.

Iyar is also the month of the quail, when God answered our hunger for meat with a gift of this rich, succulent bird. This event, which is chronicled twice in the Torah, is the subject of the second section.

The two holidays in Iyar: Pesach Sheini and Lag B'omer, are in the third and fourth sections.

MANNA: It's Raining Bread!

Manna (*mahn* in Hebrew), the miracle food of the desert, fell from the sky during the month of Iyar. We had just entered the Sinai desert; we were frightened of this huge expanse of wilderness.[3] According to Rashi (Rabbi Shlomo Yitzchaki), the food supply had been eaten.[4] We complained that we had been taken into the wilderness to die, and in response, God sent us manna.

Manna fell between a double layer of dew every morning. The first layer would evaporate when the sun came out, revealing the manna, a

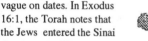
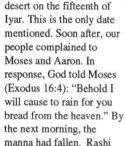

thin layer of white, frost-like food on the ground.[6] The Torah describes our awe as we gazed upon this strange new substance. We were so puzzled by what we saw that we called it manna, from the Arabic word *"mahn"* or what,[8] or from the Hebrew word for food, *"mazon"*.[9]

For the next forty years, manna was a continuous part of our lives, falling every morning, providing us with bread for the long, treacherous journey through the wilderness.

MANNA: Spiritual Test

God could have dropped loaves of bread in the desert, and the people would have been fed. But He chose to send a substance which required our participation (gathering and preparation), and a ritual process was given for its use. By following it, our ancestors proved daily that they believed in God and were committed to following His laws.[11]

Every day our people would set out at sunrise, and gather an omer (a specific measure) of manna for every person in the household.[12] The precise amount was to be gathered; neither more or less. One of the miracles of the manna was that no matter how much of it was taken, when it was brought into camp, it was the exact quantity the people should have taken.[13] They were supposed to eat it that day, and not save any for the next day's meal.[14] On Friday they harvested double what they took during the week, one portion for that day and one for the Sabbath. By noon, the manna had melted.

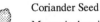
Manna: What was it?

Manna
Coriander Seed

Manna is described as a thin, scaly substance, white like coriander seed and spread over the ground like winter frost between two layers of dew.[10] Its taste has been praised in the Torah with several different descriptions. First, in Exodus 16:7, God calls it "bread from the sky," and this could refer to either its flavor or its purpose; like bread, it served as our basic food source in the desert. In Exodus 16:31, the manna tastes like wafers made of honey, while in Numbers 11:7, it looks like bdellium (a yellow fragrant flower) and tastes like a cake baked with oil. The dictionary defines it as a myrrh-like gum resin emitted from some oriental trees.

These descriptions could refer to the same food. Let us consider our sages' comments and draw a better picture of manna:

In his commentary Torah Temimah, Rabbi Baruch Halevi Epstein brings a source from the Talmud,[15] which explains that the manna tasted different depending on who ate it. The three tastes mentioned are related to the ages of those eating the manna.

Youths would taste bread; elders, oil; and babies, honey.

Rashi brings perhaps the most famous explanation. He connects the taste of the manna to Numbers 11:8, where the Torah describes the methods by which our ancestors would process the manna (grinding it in mills, beating it in mortars, cooking it in pots and making it into cakes). Rashi explains that the manna itself had no taste, but that with each preparation, its flavor would change.[16]

Nachmanides broadens the idea of a variety of tastes. In his commentary on Exodus 16:6, he cites a Talmudic source[17] which states that the manna is the bread which the angels eat. The Rabbis ask, how can the angels eat bread? Rabbi Akiva answers that the manna contained the splendor of the *shechina*. (The *shechina* is the spiritual potential of every physical thing, or the human potential to experience the divine.) Thus, Rabbi Akiva says that the manna contained the same spiritual substance and divine intervention with which the angels are sustained. Nachmanides then explains that the manna was formed from the

The commandment to eat all of the manna on the day it was gathered was an unnatural response for a nation which had endured a life of slavery, where food was an uncertain factor. Our people were entering a desert, with no idea how long the journey would last. By obeying God's law, they were showing trust in God to provide manna the next day. After a week of becoming used to the idea of not storing food, they were told to withhold part of their double portion on Friday for the Sabbath. Truly, the story of the manna reflects God's love for the Jews and their growing trust in Him.

The lesson to trust in God did not come easily to some. A few flaunted the rules and kept manna overnight. They found it spoiled and full of worms in the morning.[18] Others disobeyed Moses' injunction not to gather the manna on the Sabbath. When they went out to the fields, they found that no manna had fallen on God's day of rest.

As we celebrate the month of Iyar, may we have the same uncompromising faith that our people had so many thousands of years ago when they went out to glean the pure white manna.

MANNA: MODERN DAY EQUIVALENTS
The Tamarisk tree   Challah

Manna was a one-time miracle food; it was designed to fulfill both physical and spiritual needs. And no modern food could match its ability to become whatever the diner desired (see explanations by Rashi and Nachmanides in

85

the previous section.) Anthropologists have pinpointed one substance which seems to match the descriptions of manna in the Torah, and which has the tang of honey alluded to in Exodus 16:31. Certain scale insects which feed on the sap of the tamarisk tree produce this modern day version of manna.[19]

One of the best known Jewish traits is our tendency to incorporate reminders of the most ancient events and traditions in our daily lives, and manna is no exception. Every Friday, my mother prepares two rounded challah loaves on a platter for the Shabbat meal. The two loaves are a reminder of the double portion of manna which fell on Friday. The challah board underneath the challahs, and the covering on top, symbolize the two layers of dew which sandwiched the manna when it fell. Though manna will not be with us again until the world to come, in this world, we can still sample our Shabbat challah with a smile, and remember.[21]

QUAIL: FOOD OF WEALTH
Quail   Hunting

Does man live on bread alone? Not according to our ancestors in the desert! They complained of a lack of water, meat, fish, cucumbers, melons, leeks, onions and garlic, which they had had in Egypt.[22] But the people were not entirely without meat; they had their own flocks, which they brought with them from Egypt.[23] And for at least two times during their forty year sojourn in the desert, they also had quail.

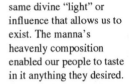

same divine "light" or influence that allows us to exist. The manna's heavenly composition enabled our people to taste in it anything they desired.

In these commentaries, manna becomes more than just food for the body. It is a sign of the high spiritual level of our forefathers, a people who merited the very fabric of the universe as food.

SOME FACTS ABOUT CHALLAH

The word "challah" comes from the biblical law in which the Jews would break off a small portion of prebaked dough and give it to their Kohanim (priests) as a weekly Sabbath offering. These and other gifts would sustain the Kohanim and enable them to devote all their time to ritual, worship, study, and Temple service. This dough had to be from wheat, barley, spelt, oat, or rye flour, and the end product had to be bread, not cake. To this day, whenever we bake bread, we set aside a portion of prebaked dough, which we burn.

The two loaves of Challah[20] are also said to be a reminder of the ritual

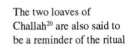

offering of challah and of the twelve showbreads of the Temple period. In the days of the Temple, twelve breads were displayed each Sabbath morning on a ritually pure table made of acacia and decorated with gold. By the next week, twelve new breads had replaced the old. The Kohanim performed the ritual of the showbreads each week in seclusion, and the recipe of these breads and their location were known only to the bakers from the house of Garmu who participated, and to the priests. Even the Talmud was unable to reveal the sumptuous details of these breads, although we do know that they were wheat and unleavened, and prepared in a hidden courtyard on Friday.

Among Sephardi Jews, two breads are the bare minimum on the Shabbat table. Some Sephardim use four breads, arranged in two pairs; the number four symbolizes the four letters of God's unpronounceable name. It also refers to the Halacha, Sephard and Ashkenaz, of having four meals on the Sabbath: Friday night dinner (for Abraham), Shabbat lunch (for Isaac), a third meal late Shabbat afternoon (for Jacob), and a post Shabbat meal (for King David).[24]

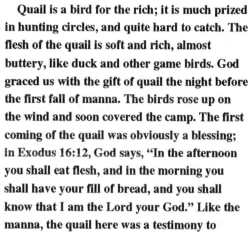

Quail is a bird for the rich; it is much prized in hunting circles, and quite hard to catch. The flesh of the quail is soft and rich, almost buttery, like duck and other game birds. God graced us with the gift of quail the night before the first fall of manna. The birds rose up on the wind and soon covered the camp. The first coming of the quail was obviously a blessing; in Exodus 16:12, God says, "In the afternoon you shall eat flesh, and in the morning you shall have your fill of bread, and you shall know that I am the Lord your God." Like the manna, the quail here was a testimony to God's ability to provide for His people.

The quail came a second time at a place called *Kivrot HaTa'avah* or the "graves of desire". The people, perhaps tired of a continuous diet of even such a wondrous food as manna, complained bitterly about their lack of meat and other foods mentioned here which they had had in Egypt. God granted them the meat in the form of quail, but here the onslaught of the quail lasted for 30 days, not one night. It was accompanied not with a vision of holiness but with a warning from God that the people had rejected Him with their pleading. The birds came on a wind from the sea, flying at chest level, so that they were easily gathered by the people. And they covered the camp, for a distance of about a day's journey on either side.[28]

In this incident, the quail are not a symbol of wealth but of overindulgence. The greediness with which the people gathered the quail through the night, spreading heaps of the bird

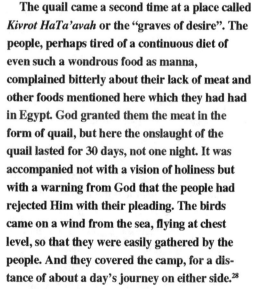

around the camp for later use, caused God to send a plague.[31] Those who ate from the quail were not even finished chewing when they died!

As we celebrate Rosh Chodesh Iyar, we should keep in mind the lessons of the quail: The first time, it was a food of wealth, a sign of God's love for his people. But there were those in Kivrot HaTa'avah who took for granted God's willingness to forgive. The quail, which before had been a sign of the bounty of the people, now symbolized our ancestors' capability to desire more than they needed, the quintessential sin of the rich man. Let us enjoy the blessings we have, and not forget that God was the one who provided them.

PESACH SHEINI
Matzoh   Cooked Eggs

On the 24th of Iyar, we celebrate "Pesach Sheini", the second Passover. In the Temple Period, those who were not ritually pure or who could not journey to Jerusalem because of the distance would not bring the Paschal sacrifice on the 14th of Nisan; the 14th of Iyar gave them a secondary day to perform the mitzvah. The Paschal Lamb was eaten on Matzot, and so today it is customary to eat a small portion of the matzoh that is left over from Passover to mark this sacrifice.[33] There is a tradition among some righteous men to eat matzot with cooked eggs and to learn the laws of Pesach Sheini on the night of the 15th of Iyar.[34]

One other reason to eat matzoh: Rav Yaakov Emdin says that in the first year of the Exodus,

Yet another Sephardi or Kabbalistic tradition is that of having twelve breads for the Sabbath, a reminder both of the twelve tribes and of the twelve showbreads.[25] Some Chasidim have challahs made of twelve balls of dough.[26]

KIVROT HATA'AVAH

Rashi points out that the people were not without meat, and brings as proof the flocks mentioned in Exodus 12:38 and the fact that the tribe of Reuven still had much in the way of cattle by the time they were ready to enter the land of Israel.[27] Instead, he says, the people were merely looking for an excuse to complain.[29] It's interesting to note that the people murmuring against God are called the *"Asafsuf,"* or the mixed multitude.[30] Rashi identifies them as a group of people who joined us when we left Egypt. They started to complain, and only then did our ancestors join in.[32]

the matzah that we took out of Egypt lasted until the 15th day of Iyar.[35]

LAG B'OMER CANDLES

On Lag B'omer, the 18th of Iyar, who can resist the tradition of lighting bonfires outdoors in the cool, spring air? A discussion of this minor but complex holiday will better illuminate the custom of kindling lights.

LAG B'OMER: RAY OF LIGHT IN DARKNESS

Lag B'omer, a day of joy in the midst of sorrow, is the 33rd day of the Omer, a 50 day period between Passover and Shavuot. As

LAG B'OMER FOOD
Barbecues
Picnics

While Lag B'omer is not associated with any particular food, many Jews celebrate the holiday outdoors, at the park or seashore. Feelings of release and thanksgiving are normal on the day of reprieve from plague. Barbecues and picnics, with hot dogs or chicken sandwhiches, are often the result.

Actually, the Omer starts with the second day of Passover, and ends with the first day of Shavuot (See Sivan).

explained in Sivan, the Omer was originally a joyful time of preparation and purification, prior to receiving the Torah. But over time, tragedies that occured during the Omer caused our Rabbis to institute certain laws of mourning. The catastrophe mentioned most is probably the death of Rabbi Akiva and his twelve thousand pairs of students. These brilliant Torah scholars died in a plague during the Omer. The Talmud tries to understand the death of so many learned scholars with this explanation: Because they did not treat each other with proper respect, they were punished.[36] Thus, we see how important it is to respect others.

The wholesale slaughter of Jewish communities through the Crusades in 1096, and the Chmielnicki massacres in 1648-9 are also supposed to have happened during the Omer.[37]

WHY CELEBRATE ON LAG B'OMER?

Lag B'omer is a special day in the middle of this devastating time. According to Eliyahu Ki Tov, Ashkenazim do not say Tachanun (a prayer of entreaty) on Lag B'omer, and they may marry or cut their hair; Sephardim observe this break on the day after. The abrogation of the laws of mourning is rooted in the tradition that the students of Rabbi Akiva ceased their dying on Lag B'omer.[38]

Another reason to celebrate on Lag B'omer: The Chatam Sofer claims that the manna fell not on the 16th of Iyar (as Rashi states) but on the 18th (Lag B'omer.) How does he reach this conclusion? He breaks up the story of manna, setting each event listed in Exodus on a different day. According to this venerated rabbi, the Jews entered the desert on the fifteenth of the month and complained on the sixteenth. God responded to their pleas on the seventeenth, and the manna fell on the eighteenth.

Lag B'omer has also been cited as the beginning of the Jewish rebellion against the Romans at the end of the Second Temple period. Josephus Flavius says that on the 17th of Iyar, Poltros, the Roman Governor, demanded 17 kikars of gold from the Jewish leaders in Jerusalem for the games in Caesarea. The next day, the rebellion began.

THE ORIGIN OF THE BONFIRE: RASHBI'S WEDDING

Rabbi Shimon Bar Yochai (Rashbi), the creator of the Zohar, the classic Jewish book on

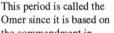

THE OMER OFFERING

This period is called the Omer since it is based on the commandment in Leviticus 23:15 to count seven weeks from the moment the Omer offering was brought, until Shavuot. The Omer offering was an omer, or one tenth of an *ephah*, of cut barley brought to the Temple on the second day of Passover. The Jews were not permitted to eat from the new grain crop until the moment the Omer was given.[39]

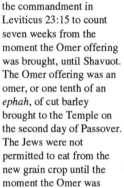

The Omer is a time of uncertainty; God judges the new crop on Passover,[40] and our people are not sure whether they will be blessed with hunger or cursed with famine in the coming year.[41] So when we count the Omer, we are always aware of the passing days of the harvest, and we pray that these days will pass in peace, for the sake of the year's crop and the health of all of Israel.

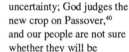
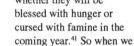

90

There are several opinions as to when the plague stopped. The M'iri, in his book *Bet Habchira*, says that Rabbi Akiva's students' deaths ceased on the thirty-third day.[43] Others, like the Maharil, write that these righteous men only died on the days that we say Tachanun, which number 32. This would exclude Passover (seven days), Rosh Chodesh Iyar (two days), Rosh Chodesh Sivan (one day), and the seven Sabbaths of the period. Thus, according to the Maharil, we celebrate on the morning after the thirty second day of the Omer.[44]

The Halacha indicates mourning only thirty-three days of the forty-nine day period. Some start this observance at the beginning of the Omer, while others begin it from Rosh Chodesh and end with Shavuot. (For more on the subject, see the Mishnah Brurahs on the Shulchan Aruch Orach Hayim §493.)

Kabbalah, died on Lag B'omer.[43] On that day, hundreds, or perhaps thousands of people journey to his grave in Meron, where he lived, and light candles or bonfires to commemorate the great light of Kabbalah that Rashbi brought to the world. Some even burn expensive clothing and material in these fires. Apparently, this is the origin of the custom of lighting bonfires on Lag B'omer.

Why rejoice on the day of the death of a righteous man? Kabbalistic tradition calls this kind of celebration a *hilula*, from the word *hallel* or praise. The meaning here is closer to *simchah* or rejoicing, and refers specifically to a wedding celebration. According to Kabbalah, the ascent of a *tzadik* (righteous one) into the highest heavens can be compared to a wedding. In this world we but gaze on the Torah's outer shell; in the world-to-come, we will perceive its light. Thus, our Rabbis compared this world to a betrothal, and the world-to-come to a marriage. The Kabbalists made this comparison for all tzadikim, but especially for Rashbi, whose book <u>The Zohar</u> revealed the inner secrets of the Torah. At his death, it is said that a light was struck, symbolizing a future world. To celebrate this "hilula" (wedding), we light candles and bonfires at his grave.[45]

THE CONTROVERSY OF MERON

According to Rabbi Ki Tov, Rashbi wants all of Israel to rejoice on the day of his death.

Rav Avraham HaLevi tells a story which proves
that we should not recite Tachanun (a prayer of
supplication) on this day. Rav Avraham kept the
custom to say Nahem (a passage of mourning
normally recited on Tisha B'av) on the
anniversary of a righteous man's death. One
Lag B'omer, he said this prayer in memory of
Rashbi. But when he finished praying, the Ari
(Rabbi Yitzchak Luria) asked him why he dared
to recite Nahem on the day of Rashbi's joy. The
Ari revealed that Rashbi had decreed that Rav
Avraham would shortly be in mourning. And
sure enough, soon afterwards, the rabbi lost his
eldest son.[46]

The celebrations for Rashbi have sparked
controversy, for it is unusual to rejoice on the
anniversary of the death of a Torah scholar.
The Chatam Sofer writes that he could not
justify instituting a holiday on a day that is not
the anniversary of a miracle, and which has not
been mentioned in the Talmud.[47] The author of
the responsa Sho'el UMeshiv objects to the
gaiety of the festivities at Rashbi's tomb. He
claims that the Ari (Rabbi Yitzchak Luria) and
his students, who began this tradition, would
celebrate in a more sober manner, with Torah
study and prayer.[48]

Others, like Rav Asher Zelig Margolies,
defend the custom. In his work Hilula
DeRashbi, Rav Margolies cites several early
sources verifying the custom of a pilgrimage to
Meron and to the tomb of Rashbi.[49]

SIVAN
(MAY-JUNE)

Torah Counting: Third Month
Regular Counting: Ninth Month

FOODS: Apples   Wine   Citron   Fish
       Water   Figs   Chicken   Meat
       Dairy Products   Wheat   Honey Cake

THEMES: Foods in Sivan: Celebrating the Torah
        Apples: Smell and Taste of the Torah
        Apples and the Tree of Knowledge
        Torah: The Spring of Life
        Shavuot Cheese
        Milk and Honey
        Rachel, the Wife of Rabbi Akiva

FOODS IN SIVAN: Celebrating The Torah

Sivan is spiritual freedom, as Nisan is release
from physical bondage. On the sixth of Sivan,
we celebrate Shavuot, the holiday of the giving
of the Torah, and much of the food of the
month reminds us of this momentous occasion.
Apples and water, two foods often compared to
Torah in the Midrash and the Talmud, will be

explained first. Perhaps the most known mouth-watering tradition for the month of Sivan is that of eating dairy products (remember Mom's light Shavuot cheesecake?) on the first day of Shavuot.[1] This custom marks our receiving the Torah, which will be described in the second section.

In Exodus 19-20 and Deuteronomy 5, the day our people accepted the Torah at Mount Sinai is described, accompanied with thunder and lightning, the physical manifestation of God, and the people's reaction. But how did we reach the level of spirituality necessary for this experience? Our ancestors were fresh from 210 years of Egyptian slavery. For all that time, they held fast to their heritage, changing neither their names nor their style of dress nor their language. Despite this identity, by the time our ancestors left Egypt, they had sunk, our sages tell us, to an extreme level of depravity. And yet, forty-nine days later, on the sixth of Sivan, the same people were ready to accept the Torah.

This is the miraculous aspect of Sivan. In the seven weeks between Passover and Shavuot, our people purified themselves, so that when the time came they were fit and prepared to accept God's gift. Thus, Shavuot is called the Feast of Weeks in remembrance of this period. It celebrates not only our delight in the Torah as a living cultural treasure, but also our role in acquiring the Torah. The event at Mount Sinai was neither one-sided nor passive; by saying *"Na'aseh v'nishmah*—we will do and we will listen," our ancestors were clearly agreeing to

THE ETROG
OR THE APPLE?

When the Talmud mentions the word "apple," does it really mean the kind of apple we now have from Washington state? According to a Tsofot on the Babylonian Talmud,[3] the Gemorrah was really talking about the *etrog*, or citron, when it claimed that the apple tree's fruit blossoms before its leaves. The citron clings to the tree from year to year, while the leaves fall off, putting the fruit before the leaves. Although the Gemorrah used the word "*tapuach*", or apple, it could very well be talking about the etrog, which is called the Adam's apple or the apple of paradise (see later section on the Tree of Knowledge). Though the etrog's fruit is bitter, it is known for its color, shape and fragrance. In fact, when the festival of Succot is over, some people preserve the etrog, stick cloves in it, and use it as a spice for the post-Sabbath Havdalah ceremony throughout the year.[4]

follow God's commandments. The statement *"Na'aseh v'nishmah"* or *"na'aseh"* appears four times in the Torah.[2] Each time, the phrase was a response to some previous agreement that God had put before the people. "We will do and we will listen" was not a statement of blind faith, but the acceptance of a contract; an avowal of commitment to God. Slaves cannot enter freely into a contract. Therefore, Sivan marks the culmination of our spiritual transformation from a slave people to a free nation. And the Torah, the treasure we received, is the spiritual food that has kept us alive for centuries.

APPLES: Smell and Taste of the Torah

The apple's delicious smell, the beauty of its natural cycle, and its sweet, sometimes tart taste, are often used in the Talmud and Midrash to praise the Torah.

The apple does not look impressive, but it <u>is</u> enticing. Its hard texture and golden or blood-red color do not hint at its juicy, sometimes sweet, sometimes tart, flavor. Similarly, God and His Torah are often underestimated in the eyes of the world. In Exodus Rabbah 17:2, the Midrash discusses this idea with the verse in Song of Songs 2:3: "As an apple tree among the trees of the wood, so is my beloved." Our Rabbis explain that though God revealed Himself to idol worshippers, they refused to accept His Torah because they did not see much use for it. However, the Jews understood the Torah's strength, and they said, "We will remain with God and with His Torah." Thus, it can be said, the Jewish people were the only ones to see beyond the apple's (or the Torah's) hard covering to the juicy pulp hidden inside.

One of the apple tree's less prized qualities is the relatively low shade level it provides, compared with other trees. This quality, too, is used to illustrate the adverse reaction of the non-Jewish world to the Torah, and the parallel acceptance of God's word by our people. In Song of Songs Rabbah 2:11, Rabbi Huna and Rabbi Atha talk about the way people shun the apple tree in the burning hot sun, because the tree provides almost no shade. So too the nations of the world refused to rest in God's shadow (protection) on the day He gave the Torah. We, however, desired His shadow, as it says in Song of Songs 2:3, "For His shadow I longed, and I sat there."

Another odd fact about the apple tree: Its fruit emerges before its blossoms. In Song of Songs Rabbah 2:11, Rabbi Aha; the son of Rabbi Zeira explains that this is a metaphor for our ancestors in Egypt. They believed in God before they heard His message, for it says, "And the people believed; and they heard that the Lord had remembered."[5] Rabbi Aha also says that our people, in receiving the Torah, were ready to act even before they had heard God's commandments, as it says "We will do and we will hear."[6]

In the aforementioned Midrash (Song of Songs Rabbah 2:11), Rabbi Azariah explains that it is fifty days from the time the apple tree

THE TREE OF KNOWLEDGE: WHAT WAS IT?

Wine	Figs
Wheat	Citron

What was the fruit of the Tree of Knowledge? We'll explore the Midrash, the Mishnah and the Gemorrah and see what they say on the subject.

The Talmud, Berachot 40a, mentions three possible foods: wine, figs, and wheat. Rabbi Meir says that the forbidden fruit was wine, since wine causes man misfortune, as it did in Genesis 9:21 when Noah planted his first vineyard and his son Ham saw him naked (See Adar: Wine: Sin and Sanctity). Rabbi Nehemiah thinks the tree was actually a fig tree. This lends a certain symmetry to the story, as afterwards Adam and Eve cover themselves with fig leaves when they realize their nakedness.[7] But Rabbi Judah's opinion is the most surprising of all. He states that the food in question was wheat, which can be considered a fruit, and he brings as proof a tradition

produces its blossoms until its fruit ripens. It was also exactly fifty days between the date we escaped from Egypt (15th of Nisan) and the date we received the Torah (6th of Sivan). In the Psikta of Rav Kahana, Rabbi Azariah says that the apple tree's fruit does not ripen until Sivan; so too the Jewish people would not give forth a fragrance to the world until Sivan. In these midrashim, the obvious regularity and the strange way in which apples grow are used to illustrate the spiritual qualities of the Torah. Also, the apple's natural heavenly fragrance is but one way in which our Rabbis showed their high regard for the Torah.

APPLES AND THE TREE OF KNOWLEDGE

The apple has long been linked by historians and theologians with the story of Adam and Eve eating from the Tree of Knowledge. However, upon close scrutiny, this link is not proven. The Bible does not name any specific fruit in the story and traditional Jewish sources do not mention an apple at all. The first one to connect the apple to Adam and Eve's sin was actually Aquila of Pontus in Asia Minor, a 2nd century convert, first to Christianity and then to Judaism, who wrote a Greek translation of the Torah. He translated Song of Songs 8:5, "I raised thee up under the apple tree; there thy mother brought thee forth," as "I raised thee up under the apple tree; there wast thou corrupted." He evidently sees the apple tree mentioned in this verse as the Tree of Knowledge. St. Jerome, who translated

97

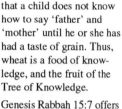

the Bible into Latin, continued this tradition, and ever since, the fruit of the Tree of Knowledge has been synonymous with the apple in the eyes of the world.[8]

APPLE CRUMBLE

My sister-in-law Gillian Solomon always serves this English dessert on Shabbat. She got it from her friend Mickey Blecher in South Africa, and has revised the recipe slightly over the years.

1 cup flour
1/2 cup sugar
1 stick (1/2 cup) margarine

Crumble these ingredients together and set aside. Line a greased dish with fruit (Partly cooked apple chunks or slices, or apple sauce) and cover with the crumble mixture. Sprinkle with cinnamon and sugar and bake for half an hour to an hour on about 300% fahrenheit or until crunchy on top.

Serve hot with fresh or pareve cream.

TORAH: THE SPRING OF LIFE
Water

What do runners drink in the middle of a race? Gatorade? Orange juice? No! The healthiest and most useful drink a runner can have is water. Ninety percent of the body is made up of water; it dissolves and transports nutrients, and moves wastes out of the body. Nobody can live long without water.[9] It is no

that a child does not know how to say 'father' and 'mother' until he or she has had a taste of grain. Thus, wheat is a food of knowledge, and the fruit of the Tree of Knowledge.

Genesis Rabbah 15:7 offers the idea that the tree in question was the etrog or citron. Why? Because in Genesis 3:6, it states, "And when the woman saw that the tree was good for food..." So Rabbi Abba of Acco says, this tree must be the citron, for that is the only tree which tastes like its fruit.

WHEAT AND TREES: HOW IS IT POSSIBLE?

How can one call wheat a tree? In Genesis Rabbah 15:7, Rabbi Zeira explains that the stalks of wheat in the Garden of Eden were tall as cedars. How, then, do we bless bread with the words "Who brings forth bread from the Earth?" Rabbi Nehemiah says that this blessing refers to the Garden of Eden, where God would grow whole loaves of bread from the ground so that Adam wouldn't have to labor for his food. Our Rabbis bring an alternative: that the blessing refers to the future Messianic era, where God will again create a world free of hard labor.

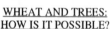

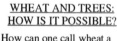

RACHEL, WIFE OF RABBI AKIVA

Rabbi Akiva's success was due to his wife, Rachel, who urged him to study Torah at the great Babylonian Academy while she worked to support him. The devotion of Rachel is evident in the Talmudic story of the night Rabbi Akiva came home after twelve years of study. One of Rachel's friends was reprimanding her for being a "living widow". But when Rachel voiced the heartfelt wish that her husband would stay and study Torah yet another twelve years, Rabbi Akiva decided to honor her words and went back to the Yeshiva. Rachel's reward came when the Rabbi returned in honor as a great Talmud chochom (learned Torah scholar) twelve years later, with thousands of followers. Poor and tattered, Rachel went to greet her husband. While his students refused to let this ragged woman near him, Rabbi Akiva recognized his wife and made them honor her. "What is yours and mine is also hers," said the Rabbi, out of love for his wife and recognition of all the sacrifices she had made for his Torah study.[11]

wonder, then, that our Rabbis compared the Torah, the wellspring of our people, to water.

Water, as a liquid, is constantly changing. It can fill a vessel of any shape, and despite its "softness", it can be very powerful. The Babylonian Talmud tells of Rabbi Akiva finding a stone with water dripping on it, where the water had bored a hole straight through the middle of the rock. This natural marvel made an impression on Rabbi Akiva. He decided that since water could bore through a rock surface, then certainly God's Torah could penetrate his head, though he was forty years old at the time and ignorant of Torah.[10] Rabbi Akiva became one of our most respected Rabbis. As we mark Rosh Chodesh Sivan, we should take pride in the Torah's spiritual strength and its ability to impact on the heart of even the most obdurate.

While water is a drink, it has many complex qualities. It can also be a destructive force, killing crops and demolishing homes in floods, and even taking lives. This dual capacity, to heal or to destroy, is connected to man's ability to choose between obedience to God's laws or alienation from them. The Yalkut Shimoni #951 says that the Torah is compared to fire,[12] water,[13] and the sword.[14] Fire can warm or destroy, water can satiate or drown, and a sword can serve as protection or as a weapon; the Torah, too, may mean life or retribution.

Water, with all its beauty and power, does not collect in a high place; it flows down from the sky as rain, to the mountains, through the valleys and hills, to the lowest point on land.

Water teaches us the lesson of humility, for as it only collects in the depths, Torah resides only in the heart of a man who is humble.[15] "Ho! All who thirst, go to water!" (Isaiah 55:1): Torah, like water, is free for all.

SHAVUOT CHEESE

Cheese	Cheese Cake	Milk

Unless you live in Wisconsin, you probably don't think much about the origins or meanings of cheese. But the Jewish tradition to eat milk products on the first day of Shavuot is rooted in both the time of year and the very nature of the holiday.

The emphasis on milk and cheese is natural for this time of year. Cows produce milk all year round, but in late May and early June, there is more cheese produced because the cows, sheep and goats have been grazing on the new spring grasses, and give more milk. It was a common practice at Spring harvest festivals worldwide to churn butter and make cheese.

But there is much more to the creamy cheese tradition than a harvest festival. The Rabbis give several different reasons for the emphasis on milk products. One explanation is that eating cheese is a reminder of the giving of the Torah. The numerical equivalent for the Hebrew word, *Chalav* or milk is 40, the same number of days that Moses stayed on Mount Sinai.[19] Also, in Psalms 68:16-17, Mount Sinai is called (among other things) a "mountain of peaks". The word for peaks, *gavnunim*, comes from the same root

THE MITZVAH OF EATING MEAT

Chicken
Meat
Fish

Yes, there is a special *minhag* (custom) of eating dairy on Shavuot. But one must still fulfill the special commandment to be happy on the holiday[16]—and being happy, according to Halacha, means eating meat. (This might pose a problem for Orthodox vegetarians.) So according to Rabbi Moshe Iserlis (the Ramah), in his commentary on the Shulchan Aruch,[17] we must eat both dairy and meat on the first day of Shavuot. We are also obligated to eat from two different breads, to commemorate the two loaves that were brought in the Temple on Shavuot.

The Mishnah Brurah[18] expands on this by explaining that one can not eat from the same loaf of bread for both dairy and meat. So is it necessary, then, to say Grace After Meals between both breads? No, says the Mishnah Brurah. The first loaf is eaten with a dairy dish (keeping the second loaf off the table so that it is not *"milchiged"*). Before cutting from the second loaf, one should eat something pareve, wash one's mouth, change tablecloths, and then put a second loaf on the table to consume.

Some Jews simplify this by eating dairy before the meal, washing, and then eating a meat meal.[20]

TWO LOAVES OF BREAD ON A FESTIVAL

On Shabbat and Yom Tov, we are also told to have two complete loaves of bread (*Lechem Mishnah*) on the table for each meal. However, we are only obligated to eat from one of the loaves.

MILK AND HONEY
Honey cake

In Song of Songs 4:11, the Torah is compared to milk and honey: "Honey and milk are under your tongue." Therefore, some Jews eat foods which have been baked or fried in honey on Shavuot.[22]

as *g'vinah* or cheese.[21] So when you sink your teeth into a piece of cheddar on Shavuot, think of the miracles God performed on Mount Sinai.

There are other reasons to connect cheese with Mount Sinai. One rabbinic tradition relates that by the time our people had finished receiving the law at Mount Sinai, their milk had turned sour and was on its way to becoming cheese!

The best reason I could find is that when our people received the Torah, they were suddenly obligated to observe the laws of Kashruth. Beforehand, they had been allowed to eat non-kosher meat, or meat that was not slaughtered properly. But now they had to make their dishes kosher (a job and a half!). They could not do so until after the holiday of Shavuot had passed, so, for expediency, they ate a simple milk meal. And now, so do we.[23]

BROCCOLI-SPINACH CHEESE LOAF

2 7-1/2 oz packages farmer cheese
3 eggs
2 packages frozen vegetables: 1 chopped broccoli, 1 chopped spinach
3 tbsp. margarine
3-4 tbsp. wheat germ
Mrs. Dash seasoning (to taste)

Mix all ingredients together. Oil 9 1/4 by 6 1/2 inch loaf pan. Put mixture in pan and top with wheat germ for a crust. Bake at 350 degrees for 1 to 1 1/4 hours (cover for first 45 minutes, and then uncover for rest of baking time).

—*Toby Solomon*

MELK TERT
(Milk Tart: South African traditional dessert)

2 cups milk	1 egg
1 1/2 tbsp. flour	1 1/2 tbsp. corn starch
1/2 cup sugar	1 tsp. vanilla

Mix into a smooth paste: egg, flour, corn starch, sugar and vanilla. Set aside. Bring milk to a boil. Turn milk off and wait a few seconds. Pour paste into milk and stir until thickens like custard. (Note: Sometimes it's necessary to put the mixture back on the heat for it to thicken.) Pour immediately over a dish that has been lined with tea biscuits. Sprinkle with cinnamon and refrigerate. Serve cold, and enjoy!

—*Mickey Blecher*

Hebrew shekel, 66 B.C., showing pomegranates

Coin of Agrippas I, depicting grain

Biblical spies in Jericho returning with cluster of grape vine

Coin of the Bar Koch[ba] Uprising 132-5 CE showing fig tree

TAMMUZ
(JUNE-JULY)

Torah Counting: Fourth month
Regular Counting: Tenth month

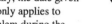

FIRST OR SECOND?

Actually, the date given here only applies to Jerusalem during the Second Temple Era. In the First Temple period, the walls were broken on the 9th. Our sages could have burdened us with <u>two</u> fasts in one week. Instead, they chose the date from the Second Temple because the loss is felt more keenly, since we have not yet returned to build a third Temple.

The other three fasts are: The Fast of Gedaliah (the 3rd of Tishrei), the Tenth of Tevet, and the Ninth of Av. (See chapters on Tevet and Av.)[2]

Themes: The Seventeenth of Tammuz
           Other Tragedies
           The Three Weeks

The Seventeenth of Tammuz

The seventeenth of Tammuz marks the day that the Romans breached the walls of Jerusalem. We fast from morning until night to commemorate those cracks in the wall. This fast is just one of four[1], a cycle reminding us of the destruction of both Temples and of the Jewish commonwealth.

On the seventeenth of Tammuz, a city which had been for centuries praised and admired by the nations of the world, became just another city to be plundered. The culture of Temple Judaism, now lost in the mists of time, will remain so until the days of the Messiah.

OTHER TRAGEDIES

In the Babylonian Talmud, Ta'anit 26[3], our sages credit the seventeenth of Tammuz with these misfortunes:

1) Moses came down from Mount Sinai, saw the people sinning with the worship of the Golden Calf, and broke the first tablets of the law.[4] These tablets, written in fire by God's hand, were holier than the second ones, which were written by Moses. The destruction of the first tablets signifies the breaking of the covenant with God after only forty days. By committing idol worship, one of the Torah's most serious sins, our people had marred what was earlier a pure covenant. The shattering of the tablets echoes the devastation of Moses' hopes for his people.

2) On this day, the sacrifices ceased in the First Temple. The animal supply ran out long before, but the daily Tamid Sacrifice had continued for a while because of the Romans. They would send two sheep over the wall of the city in exchange for gold. Finally, on the seventeenth of Tammuz, they sent up two pigs, which are impure and cannot be sacrificed. The pigs, however, pushed against the wall when they were halfway up and fell 40 parsahs (a measurement). From that moment, the sacrifices stopped.[7]

3) Apustumus the wicked burned the Torah.[8] According to later scholars, this event occurred about sixteen years before the Jewish rebellion against the Romans, during the time of Comenus, a Roman curator. Josephus states that Comenus burned the Torah after Stephanus, a royal official, was robbed on the

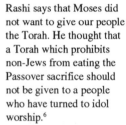

Even though these tablets were written by God, Moses did not hesitate to break them. He was angry at the sins of his people, who had not kept their promise ("*Na'aseh V'nishmah*- we will do and we will hear.")[5]

Rashi says that Moses did not want to give our people the Torah. He thought that a Torah which prohibits non-Jews from eating the Passover sacrifice should not be given to a people who have turned to idol worship.[6]

road, to punish the Jewish community. (Stephanus is a variant on the name Apustumus.)[9]

4) An image (or idol) was placed in the Sanctuary. Rashi says that Menasseh, a Judean king (532-477 BCE), was the culprit;[10] others cite Apustumus.[11]

A LENIENT FAST

The seventeenth of Tammuz is a more lenient fast than the 9th of Av. Jewish law permits us to wash, to anoint ourselves and to wear leather shoes. Sick people, pregnant women and nursing mothers need not fast if they feel the affliction. But our sages cautioned those who don't fast to avoid eating sumptuous meals; simple fare is the watchword on this day of introspection and repentance.

THE THREE WEEKS

It took the Romans three weeks to push their way to the Temple and burn it down. Today those three weeks are a solemn time, and the laws of mourning are in effect. So from the seventeenth of Tammuz to the ninth of Av, you won't usually see much rejoicing in the Jewish community; weddings are not held, music and dancing are prohibited. Trips to the barber are not allowed in the Ashkenazi community, although Sephardim allow hair cutting until the week of the 9th of Av.

These three weeks have historically been unlucky, so our sages warn us to avoid long journeys during this period, a time called *ben hamitzarim*, or "between the narrow straits." from "All her pursuers caught her between the narrow straits."[12] The image, written by the prophet Jeremiah, evokes a feeling of pursuit; indeed, the Three Weeks are bounded by two times of trouble (*metzar*): the 17th of Tammuz and the 9th of Av.

AV
(JULY-AUG.)

Torah Counting: Fifth Month
Regular Counting: Eleventh Month

Foods: Eggs   Lentils   Ashes

Themes: Av: Month of Mourning
           The Nine Days
           Tisha B'Av (The Ninth of Av)
           Seudah Mafseket (The Meal of Cessation)
           Foods of Mourning

AV: MONTH OF MOURNING

The first nine days of Av cast a shadow on
the rest of the month. They are devoted to
remembering Jerusalem: the city in its glory,
the city in its downfall. Such a difference
between the two! The traditions that have been
passed down to us speak of a sorrow so deep
that none can assuage. "If I forget thee,
Jerusalem, let my right hand forget its
movement. Let my tongue cleave to its palate, if
I do not remember you, if I do not raise
Jerusalem above my highest joy."[3]

MENACHEM AV

In Av, God's sorrow is so
great that He is like a father
(Av) who must be
comforted (*menachem*).
Therefore, the month of Av
is also called *Menachem
Av*.[1]

ROSH HODESH:
A FAST OF
REMEMBRANCE

Rosh Hodesh Av is the day
on which Aaron the Priest
died; though Rosh Hodesh
is supposed to be a happy
occasion, some fast on
Rosh Hodesh Av in
memory of Aaron.[2]

Even at weddings we remember Jerusalem. When the groom breaks the glass, he symbolically raises Jerusalem above the happiest day of his life.

* quite unlike the *Seudah Mafseket* before Yom Kippur!

It has been suggested that eating two types of food is the way of happiness.[5]

HEIGHTENING THE SORROW: FROM BUYING TO WASHING

From the three weeks on, we can't eat new fruits (fruits that we haven't eaten in a year) or buy new clothes; but from Rosh Hodesh Av, it is prohibited to wash one's clothing (which sends observant women hurrying to do the household laundry before the nine days).[7]

Sephardic custom prohibits meat only on the week of Tisha B'Av.

Even in the midst of this most terrible tragedy, the Jewish penchant for food plays its part. Before Tisha B'Av (the ninth of Av), we eat a meal called the *Seudah Mafseket* (The Meal of Cessation). But this pre-fast meal could not be called a feast; it is a simple, sedate meal*, so solemn that it is only supposed to include one *tavshil* (prepared food- more on that later.)[4] It is as if the tragic feeling of Tisha B'Av reaches out to affect even the meal before, and the custom is to eat foods of mourning: lentils or eggs, and ashes (see section on the Seudah Mafseket.)

This chapter will deal mostly with the foods of the Seudah Mafseket; even if you can't enjoy the foods on this Rosh Hodesh Av, you can at least savor the spirituality embodied in all of our customs, whether happy or sad.

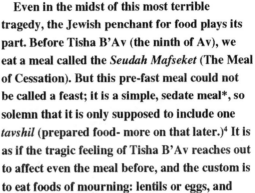

THE NINE DAYS

From Rosh Hodesh Av until Tisha B'Av, we enter a more heightened period of mourning. It is customary to abstain from eating meat and drinking wine, in remembrance of the destruction of the Holy Temple. Meat and wine are foods of happiness, and remind us of the sacrifices and wine libations which have ceased with the destruction of the Temple.[6]

It is customary to prohibit swimming during the nine days. The sweltering heat of late summer makes this perhaps one of the hardest laws of the nine days to fulfill. There are two reasons for prohibiting swimming (although there may be others). The first reason, and that

which is most often cited, is that the Nine Days are a dangerous time for our people. Accidents happen near water; we don't want to put ourselves at risk.

This law more likely falls under the category of a restriction of pleasure during a period of mourning. For instance, we are not allowed to bathe for pleasure during the nine days, but we can take showers for health reasons.[8] Swimming is essentially a form of recreation, and is therefore forbidden. Perhaps that's why many Orthodox day camps allow only instructional swimming during the Nine Days.

TISHA B'AV (THE NINTH OF AV)

On Tisha B'Av, the Romans (and the Babylonians in the First Temple period) finally made their way to the Temple, and set it on fire.[9] While the Temple was standing, it testified that God was in our midst. This is also the meaning of the verse "build me a house and I shall dwell amongst them."[10] But when the Temple was destroyed, a pillar of our existence was shattered. No longer could we be sure of God's comforting presence. We were like a child who had been told that his father no longer wanted him at his table. The blow we were dealt transcends the ages; we should feel it when we fast through the night and day of Tisha B'av.

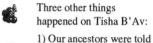

TRAGEDIES OF TISHA B'AV

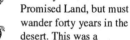

Three other things happened on Tisha B'Av:

1) Our ancestors were told that they could not enter the Promised Land, but must wander forty years in the desert. This was a punishment for listening to the spies, who had reported that the land of Israel was unconquerable. Our sages say that they cried that night out of a loss of faith; God gave them a reason to cry for generations.[11]

2) About 52 years after the destruction of the Second Temple, Beitar, the stronghold of Bar Kochba's rebellion, was captured, and tens of thousands of Jews were killed.[12]

3) Turnus Rufus razed the remains of the Second Temple, so that it would not be rebuilt.[13]

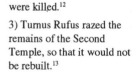

SEUDAH MAFSEKET
(THE MEAL OF CESSATION)

The last meal before Tisha B'Av is far from a banquet. Hot meats and wines of any color are persona non grata; fancy dishes like succulent linguini or spicy souffle should not be on the table.

Chicken and fish are also prohibited, for, like meat, they induce happiness.

What foods <u>are</u> allowed at the Seudah Mafseket? Jewish law does not allow more than one *tavshil* (prepared food). So having two kinds of food on your table is not good. What is considered a *tavshil* is a matter of involved debate.

Raw fruits and vegetables are permitted in unlimited quantities, because they are not in the category of "tavshil".[14] Neither is cheese, butter and margarine.[15]

It is of utmost importance that when making your Seudah Mafseket, you don't accidentally include more than one *tavshil*. It is easier than you might think to slip. For instance, a vegetarian stew might have several different kinds of vegetables: potatoes, carrots, and some lima beans. Three foods, three *tavshils,* right? Not necessarily. The key question here is whether or not the foods in question are normally eaten as one dish. If they are, then the dish is considered one *tavshil,* but if they aren't, it would be three: the potatoes, the carrots, and the lima beans. However, while a huge cholent might technically be considered one *tavshil,* it would probably be too festive to include in the Seudah Mafseket.

The Beis Yoseph, compiler of the Shulchan Aruch, gives as an example a dish of lentils, onions, and eggs, which was apparently regularly eaten in his time.[16]

Two pots worth of one *tavshil* is treated as two tavshils.[17] The Mishnah Brurah explains that this refers to the quantity of food prepared; you should not cook more than the participants can eat at one meal.[18]

How is it possible to make a Seudah Mafseket consisting of one *tavshil,* and still feed your family enough to strengthen them before the fast? Well, you can eat a nice plate of fruits and vegetables for starters. And there's nothing limiting the amount of your chosen *tavshil,* as long as you don't reach the point of gluttony (hence the two-pot rule mentioned above).

But Ashkenazi families customarily eat a meal before Minchah (the afternoon prayer) to properly fortify themselves. This meal can have a few courses as long as it's not the last meal before the fast. Later, after minchah, the real Seudah Mafseket is eaten.[20]

Technically, it's possible to cook two pots worth of food, and have one person eat from each pot.[19]

FOODS OF MOURNING
Eggs   Lentils   Ashes

When mourners come back from a funeral, they sit on low chairs and eat a meal. We symbolize our mourning over the First and Second Temples at the Seudah Mafseket by sitting on the floor, or on a low chair, and eating these foods of mourning.[21] The most common custom is to eat bread and a hard boiled egg. At the end of the meal, one dips a piece of bread in ashes and says, "This is the Tisha B'Av meal."[22]

The Shulchan Aruch speaks of the custom of eating an egg and lentil dish for the Seudah Mafseket; apparently, this was common in his time.[23] According to Rabbi Zinger,

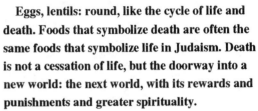

this is a problem, because the eggs and lentils are considered two separate tavshils.[24]

LENTILS: ESAU'S TRADE

Esau, Jacob's brother, sold his birthright for some of Jacob's homemade lentil soup. Why lentils? Abraham had just died, and Jacob was cooking the soup as a food of mourning. Esau was tired and hungry from a day of hunting— the rest is history![25]

Ovals are better at distributing force than most shapes. How durable are eggs? A chicken's egg was dropped 183 meters from a helicopter and survived, and an ostrich egg can withstand the weight of a 115 kilogram man. How's that for the Guinness Book of World Records?[27]

BEGINNINGS AND ENDINGS

Eggs, lentils: round, like the cycle of life and death. Foods that symbolize death are often the same foods that symbolize life in Judaism. Death is not a cessation of life, but the doorway into a new world: the next world, with its rewards and punishments and greater spirituality.

The egg is a womb, protecting the life inside. The shape of the egg gives it the strength to withstand the pressure of a mother hen.[26] And the hen sitting on her baby's eggs warms the life inside, keeping the temperature of this external womb constant. Hens know to turn their eggs around, and exactly when to do it, to help the chick inside grow and mature. At the end of the incubation period, this marvel called an egg is broken open from the inside, and a new life appears. But if the chick cannot break through, or if the egg has never been fertilized, what could have been a womb becomes instead a tomb, a depository of lost life potential.[28]

Do you wonder that eggs are eaten by mourners? They remind the mourner that life and death are two sides of the same coin. The mourner is surrounded by death, but the egg is a poignant reminder that life goes on. On Tisha B'Av, the spiritual loss that we suffer may throw us into the blackest despair. Yet the egg comforts us with the knowledge that Jewish life continues, even without the Holy Temple. It brings us hope that God will speedily redeem us with the Messiah, in our time.

....

ELUL
AUG.-SEPT.

Torah Counting: Sixth month
Regular Counting: Twelfth month

Foods: Salt   Mustard   Knives   Challah

Themes: Month of Teshuvah
           The Ram's Horn
           A Long Tradition
           Teshuvah and Sacrifice
           Salt on the Altar
           The Table is an Altar

ELUL: OUT WITH THE OLD,
IN WITH THE NEW

In Elul, we begin a process of self-examination
which lasts from Rosh Hodesh until Yom
Kippur (the Tenth of Tishrei). We ask ourselves:
How did we fare this year? The last eleven
months have provided us with opportunities to
do mitzvot and to sin. Which path did we
choose? Have we lived up to our potential? How
would we change ourselves for the better?[1]

This process of teshuvah (repentance) begins
in Elul. Teshuvah is not mere cerebral
reflection; it is a thorough transformation of

A LONG TRADITION

The forty days between
Rosh Hodesh Elul and Yom
Kippur have been days of
reconciliation since the time
of Moses. The start of this
tradition was Moses' second
ascent of Mount Sinai on
Rosh Hodesh Elul. In the
aftermath of the Golden
Calf, he climbed Mount
Sinai to pray for forgiveness
for our people. He stayed
there for forty days, and
descended on Yom Kippur,
having secured God's mercy
and the second set of tablets.
These are days of Divine
Mercy, and therefore
especially appropriate for
teshuvah.[2]

the soul, a difficult and time-consuming activity. By starting our teshuvah in Elul, we allow ourselves sufficient time to do it right. Many of Elul's customs are designed to help us to do teshuvah. We recite *Selichot* (prayers for forgiveness) during Elul (see sidebar) and we add Psalm 27 to the morning and evening prayers until Hoshana Rabbah. Throughout the month of Elul, we blow the shofar (Ram's horn) four times a day. This is meant to awaken our hearts, to call us to teshuvah.[3]

The forty-day cycle of teshuvah is just one more sign that the Jewish calendar is not linear. Elul, the last month of the old year and Tishrei, the first of the New Year, are tied together in a loop of repentance and renewal. Each year is not its own entity; it is connected to the year ahead and the year before. The past touches the present, which grips the future, as if the Jewish life cycle were one long, rich tapestry. Yet the lesson of Elul is that the sins of the past do not have to stain the hopes of the future. God's ear is always open, and He is always willing to forgive.

TESHUVAH AND SACRIFICE

Doing teshuvah is not the only method of earning a better fate. Today, we have two more: tefillah (prayer) and tsedakah (charity). The latter two do not, however, have the scope of teshuvah, which addresses sins committed against God alone, as well as those directed against other human beings.

But in the Temple period, we had yet another

---

eshuvah literally means return," and it involves a enewal of commitment to God. By sinning, we have een denying the truth of God's Torah. Now we are eturning to Him as a son or daughter may reconcile vith a father after long ears of estrangement.

Some say Selichot hroughout the month of Elul, except for Rosh Hodesh and Shabbat. Others say them from the fifteenth of Elul. The Ashkenazic custom is to say Selichot from the Sunday of the week of Rosh Hashanah (but not less than four days before the holiday.)[4]

SHOFAR: THE RAM'S HORN

The shofar, blown throughout the month of Elul, should rouse the sinner's conscience. Maimonides notes: "...it contains an allusion: Awake you slumberers, arise from your slumber - examine your deeds, repent and remember your Creator."[5] But the shofar has a second purpose, to instill fear in the hearts of those who hear it. Amos

method of serving God, one which is hard for us to appreciate: sacrifices. Far from cruel acts of barbarism, these rituals were designed to teach humility and holiness. A participant or observer who had no emotional reaction to a sacrifice missed the entire point of the ritual.[9]

Seeing an animal dying, its blood flowing, brought a realization of one's own mortality.[10] In addition, these offerings illustrated God's role as a kind ruler. Sacrificing an animal makes one more conscious of God's tremendous mercy in sustaining us. He could easily take back His gift of life; yet he continually provides air to breathe, food to eat, and plants and animals for our benefit.

Many sacrifices, individual and collective, had an element of atonement. *Viduy*, or confession, was an integral part of the ceremony for such sacrifices as the sin (*chata'at*) and guilt (*asham*) offerings. Other sacrifices were voluntary gifts of thanksgiving to God, and usually involved words of praise.[11]

In Elul, a month of service to God,* it is appropriate to discuss some foods used in the Temple ceremonies, and the customs which have evolved from these services.

SALT ON THE ALTAR

By law, every sacrifice, whether animal, bird, or flour, had to be salted. According to <u>Sefer Hachinuch</u>, a Kohen (Priest) would salt both sides of the animal, although it was considered kosher after the fact even if it had

the prophet mentions this (Amos 3:6) in his question to the people: "Will a shofar be sounded in the city and the people not quake?"[6]

The text of "Unitanah Tokef", a Rosh Hashanah prayer (see Tishrei) reads: "But repentance, charity, prayer and charity remove the evil of the decree."[7] The Babylonian Talmud adds a fourth way: that of changing one's name.[8]

Viduy (confession) has always been a private thing between a person and his maker. Yet by law, *viduy* on Yom Kippur must be said out loud, so that the speaker can hear. According to the Talmud, every Yom Kippur we squeezed into the Ezras Yisroel (Courtyard of Israel) for the day's service. At one point, we prostrated ourselves on the ground and confessed our sins. To give us privacy for viduy, God miraculously put four amot (app. 6-8 feet) of space between each person![12]

* when we blow the ram's horn, a reminder of Isaac's sacrifice.

SALT: LASTING PURITY

Salt symbolizes permanence. For instance, a "covenant of salt" is a lasting treaty; In II

Chronicles 13:5, Aviah, King of Judah, refers to King David's House as a "Covenant of Salt", in that God said that his line would rule even in the time of the Messiah.[13] To this day, we traditionally bring bread and salt to a new home to signify our hope for permanence and blessing.[14]

Salt was also a purifying agent. In kashering, it is used to draw out the blood from the meat. Many cultures preserved and flavored their food with this nutrient, so necessary to the human body's delicate balance.[17]

been salted somewhat. The salting occurred in three places: in a special Salting Courtyard, where a Kohen would salt the limbs of each animal, on the ramp of the altar, and on top of the altar itself, where the Minchahs (meal offerings) and frankincense were salted before they were burned.[15]

The salting of the sacrifices is called a "Covenant of Salt" in the Torah[16] because of the Midrashic story of the covenant that God made with the earthly waters. On the second day of creation, God split the heavenly waters and the earthly waters, creating the sky and the sea. The lower waters complained that they wished to be closer to God. To address this inequality, He promised that salt, which comes from the sea, would be a prominent part of the Temple service, and that water would be poured on the altar on Shemini Azeret[18] (See Tishrei: Nisuch Hamayim-The Water Libation). Thus, the lower waters gained in spirituality. By salting an offering, we not only obeyed the law, but we also became a part of this ancient covenant.

According to Nachmanides, this Covenant of Salt teaches us that the altar service, like salt, could be destructive or helpful. Salt prevents plants from growing, and it can be corrosive, but it also preserves food. If performed properly and sincerely, the altar service preserved us; if neglected, it could bring destruction and exile.[19]

The preservative qualities of salt signify the longevity of our people. The services that we performed for God in the Temple protected our souls.[20] In addition, salt made the offerings more important to those bringing them.[21] For salt has historically been a symbol of permanence, used for purity and consecration, and a chosen flavoring on food *(See sidebar: Salt: Lasting Purity)*.

THE TABLE IS AN ALTAR
Salt   Mustard
S'micha (The Placing of Hands)
Challah

Our food customs and laws often serve to remind us of the Temple services. As our Rabbis have said, "The table is like an altar and the meal an offering."[22] Eating gives one strength to serve God. Therefore, many of the sacrificial laws are the basis for the customs of the Jewish table.

We wash our hands for bread for two reasons: to remember the *T'rumah* (a special gift offering for the Kohen), and as a matter of cleanliness and purity. The Kohanim would wash before eating the *T'rumah* to purify themselves. The rest of our people were then commanded to wash before eating bread, to keep the practice in the minds of the Kohanim. Today, in the absence of Temple and *T'rumah*, the practice of washing for bread continues, a reminder of the past, and a continuation of our pursuit of purity.

We dip our bread into salt or some other condiment at every meal*, to recall the salting of the offerings.[23] And as the Temple offerings protected us with the merit of the "Covenant of Salt", the salting of the bread protects us from

* By Jewish law, a meal must contain bread. The Shulchan Aruch suggests mustard as an alternative, but most Ashkenazic homes use salt, which directly relates to the sacrifices.[24] On Rosh Hashanah, honey is the spread of choice. (See Tishrei.)

The Magen Avraham mentions a Kabbalistic teaching that it is a mitzvah to dip the bread in the salt instead of pouring the salt on the bread. For bread is a mercy to man, and thus symbolizes the quality of

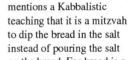
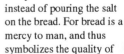

116

mercy. Salt is sharp and alludes to the quality of judgment. When the bread is on top, we are showing that mercy has overcome strict judgment.[25]

* *S'micha* was only required for individual sacrifices, with the exception of these three: *Bechor* (the firstborn), *Ma'aser* (a tithe of 1/10 of one's produce) and the Paschal Lamb (See Nisan).

suffering. For when we wash our hands, we must often wait for others to finish washing and join us at the table before making a Motzi. We have not yet completed the mitzvah and are waiting, doing nothing, and so we are particularly vulnerable to the Satan's machinations. And as we've already noted (in Tishrei: Kreplach: the Hidden Moon and accompanying sidebar), the Satan is always ready to incite us to sin. But again, bringing the salt to the table elevates the simple act of eating, and makes it a holy act, like the sacrifices of old.[26]

It is customary to place one's hands on the bread when saying the Motzi,[27] a reminder of the ritual of *S'micha*, the placing of hands. The individual bringing a sacrifice would place two hands between the horns of the animal*, and state the purpose of the sacrifice. For sin and guilt offerings, which were brought as atonement, he would recite *viduy*; if the sacrifice was voluntary, he might praise God.[28] Our sages also tell us to raise the loaf when we say God's name in the blessing; on Shabbat, when we eat two loaves, we raise them both.[29]

Even when we've finished our meal, and are ready to bensch (recite Grace After Meals), the altar metaphor continues. Now we must remove all knives from the table, in commemoration of the building of the altar. For King Solomon could not put any metal to the stones which would become the Temple altar; instead, he had a special worm called the *shamir*, which could cut through stone![30]

For Recipes, see Recipe Reference.

THE ROSH HODESH TABLE

N O T E S

KEY: *BT = Babylonian Talmud*
          JT = Jerusalem Talmud
          MB = Mishnah Brurah
          MT = Mishnah Torah (Maimonides' Code of Jewish Law)
          ShA = Shulchan Aruch OCh = Orach Chaim YD = Yoreh De'ah
              (parts of the Shulchan Aruch)
          SeHat = Sefer HaToda'ah (Eng. Ed. of Sehat)
          BOH = The Book of Our Heritage

PREFACE

1. Arlene Agus, "This Month is For You: Observing Rosh Hodesh as a Woman's Holiday," Elizabeth Koltun, Jewish Women, New Perspectives. N.Y.: Schocken Publishers, 1986, p. 88.
2. See section on The Sun and the Moon in the Leap Month chapter.
3. See Tishrei.
4. Where the holiday of Rosh Hashanah takes precedence (see Tishrei.)
5. See Nisan.
6. Midrash Pirkei De Rabbi Eliezer, Chap. 45, and Mekore Haminhagim, No. 38.
7. Rashi, Megillah, see Agus, p. 86.
8. See Agus, ibid., pp. 87-88.
9. We learn of this custom from King Saul, who held Rosh Hodesh banquets.
10. Agus, ibid., p. 86, quoting Or Zorua.
11. BT, Hullin 60a. For more on this, see Leap Month chapter (Adar Beit).
12. Pirkei De Rabbi Eliezer, Chap. 51; Also Midrash Konen pp. 25-26.
13. Sefer Hemdat Hayamim, Vol. 1, p. 25. Also Pirke De Rabbi Eliezer, Chap.
45. Arlene Agus suggests that this means women will be equal to men in status without becoming identical in character (Agus, ibid., p. 86.)
14. Information on the history of Rosh Hodesh taken from Agus, ibid., pp. 85-89.
15. This was suggested by Linda Safron, organizer of a Rosh Hodesh group.
16. Phone interview with Sally Rappeport, end January, 1995.
17. Phone interview with Linda Safron, 3rd week of January, 1995.
18. The precise time that the New Moon appears in Jerusalem.
19. When the moon is at its fullest.
20. If there is no minyan, one can say it with three men or alone (The Complete Artscroll Siddur. Rabbi Nosson Scherman and Rabbi Meir Zlotowitz, eds. N.Y.: Mesorah Publications, 1985; 1989; 1992; p. 613).
21. Information on Kiddush Levana from The Complete Artscroll Siddur, pp. 612-613, 453.
22. Phone interview with Linda Safron, third week of January 1995.

<u>TISHREI</u>

1. BT, Rosh Hashanah 16a.
2. <u>The Complete Artscroll Machzor</u>, Rosh Hashanah ed., Nusach Ashkenaz.
N.Y.: Mesorah Pub., 1985, Rabbi Nosson Scherman, Tr., Rabbi Meir Zlotowitz,
co-editor, p. 483.
3. *Nehemiah* 8:10.
4. MB No. 1 to ShA OC §597; also see BT Rosh Hashanah 8a. Cited by Rabbi
Chaim Nussbaum, <u>The Essence of Teshuvah: A Path to Repentance</u>. N.J.: Jason
Aronson Inc., 1993, pp. 132-3.
5. *Leviticus* 16:29, 16:31, 23:27, 23:32 and Numbers 29:7.
6. For more information, see MB on ShA §611-15.
7. Based on *Leviticus* 23:42: "In the Succot you shall dwell for seven days." The
BT, Sukah 28b, states that one dwells in the succah as one dwells in one's house,
which includes eating, drinking, and sleeping; also see MB on ShA, §639.)
8. Nussbaum, ibid., p. 139.
9. Rabbi Joseph Dov Soloveitchik, <u>On Repentance</u>. Jerusalem: World Zionist
Org., 1975, pp. 44-45.
10. See Elul.
11. Rav Yochanan in the BT, Rosh Hashanah, 16B.
12. MT, Laws of Teshuvah, Chap. 3.
13. Eliyahu Ki Tov, <u>The Book of Our Heritage</u>. Tr. from Hebrew <u>Sefer
Hatoda'ah</u> by Nathan Bulman. N.Y.: Feldheim Publishers, 1978, vol. 1, p. 25.
14. MT, Laws of Teshuvah 3:4.
15. *Deuteronomy* 8:8.
16. BT, Kiddushin 20a.
17. The extent of the person's gain in learning depends (in the passage) on the
amount of Torah he already has acquired. A Torah scholar is said to gain in
learning, and a plain man will gain greater accomplishment in the
commandments.
18. Song of Songs 4:3: "Thy temples are like a pomegranate split open." Here
the nation of Israel is being compared by the author to a person, whose temples
are full of seeds like a pomegranate (and thus with Torah).
19. Songs of Songs Rabbah, IV, ii, 1.
20. Rabbi Yehuda Dov Zinger, *Ziv Haminhagim* (Heb.). Jerusalem: Dror
Publishing, 1971, p. 172.
21. Zinger, ibid., p. 172. Tr. of Micah from Rabbi A. J. Rosenberg, <u>The Book of
the Twelve Prophets, Vol. Two</u>. N.Y.: Judaica Press, 1988, p. 236.
22. Ki Tov, ibid., pp. 177-8.
23. Ki Tov, ibid., p. 178.
24. Ki Tov, ibid., pp. 177-8.
25. ibid.
26. JT, Sukah, Chap. 5.

27. *Isaiah* 12:3.
28. From the Jerusalem Bible: The Holy Scriptures. Jerusalem: Koren Pub., 1989, p. 490.
29. Ki Tov, ibid., p. 178.
30. BT, Rosh Hashanah 16b.
31. Pinchus Kahati, Kahati Edition, Mishnah Seder Mo'ed, Rosh Hashanah 1:2. Jerusalem: Haichal Shlomo, 1992, pp. 198-9.
32. MT, Book of Love, Laws of Prayer, Chap. 1, § 4, §5 and §6.
33. Ki Tov, ibid., p. 211. From the Mishnah, Seder Mo'ed, Rosh Hashanah 1:2.
34. *Pirkei Avot* (Sayings of The Fathers) 3:17
35. *Leviticus* 26.
36. Ki Tov, ibid., p. 211.
37. ibid.
38. *Exodus* 23:16.
39. Ki Tov, ibid., p. 211.
40. ibid.
41. The custom of *Y'hi Ratzon* is based in two Talmudic sources. In the BT, Horayot 12a and Critut 6a, Abaye is quoted as saying that since signs have substance, it is customary to eat gourds, carrots, leeks, spinach and dates on Rosh Hashanah. The ShA OC, §583, expands on this list.
42. Artscroll *Machzor, Rosh Hashanah,* p. 97.
43. Zinger, ibid., p. 155.
44. Translation from The Artscroll Tehillim (Psalms), tr. and annot. by Rabbi Hillel Danziger with Rabbi Nosson Scherman. N.Y.: Mesorah Pub., 1988, p. 179.
45. This explanation by Rabbi Nosson Scherman in The Complete Artscroll Machzor: Rosh Hashanah, p. 99, in the name of the Biyur HaGra, and the Maharal (as cited by the Darchei Moshe.)
46. MB 1 on ShA OC §583.
47. For these and other examples, see ShA §583 and accompanying Mishnah Brurahs.
48. ShA §583 No. 2 (and accompanying MBs); Artscroll Machzor for Rosh Hashanah (quoting the Magen Avrohom on p. 99); Zinger, ibid., p. 155).
49. Based on the text in *Deuteronomy* 28:13: "And Hashem shall place you as the head and not as the tail." (Onkeles interprets: "as a mighty one and not as a weakling.") (The Complete Artscroll Machzor: Rosh Hashanah, pp. 99-100, quoted from the Magen Avrohom.)
50. "Food," Encyclopedia Judaica, Vol. 9.
51. A ram was provided by God in place of Isaac (Genesis 22:13).
52. MB No. 7 on ShA §583 No. 2.
53. Zinger, ibid., p. 155.
54. Rabbi Moses of Premisla, Mateh Moshe. Jerusalem: 1984, Part 5, pp. 160-61.
55. See sidebar "Carrots And Rubia: By Any Name".

56. Rabbi Moshe Iserlis (The Ramah), in his commentary on the ShA §583.

57. Ramah, ibid.

58. At first glance, the two are not equivalent, as the aleph in the word *cheit* makes it worth one more than *egoz*. Rabbi Zinger explains that this aleph does not count because it isn't pronounced (Zinger, p. 155).

59. Rabbi Zinger quotes this as the main reason behind the custom (Zinger, ibid).

60. *I Samuel* 25:5-11.

61. Cited by Rashi and Ralbag, inferred from the words of a youth to Abigail (I Samuel 25:14-17): "They were a wall over us both night and day..." (From The Book of Samuel I, Rabbi A. J. Rosenberg, Tr. N.Y.: The Judaica Press, 1988.)

62. *I Samuel* 16:13.

63. BT, Sanhedrin 36a.

64. *I Samuel* 25:38: "And it was just ten days after, that the Lord inflicted a stroke on Nabal, and he died (The Book of Samuel, Judaica Press ed., p. 216)." Both Rashi and Radak state that these ten days were the Ten Days of Repentance between Rosh Hashanah and Yom Kippur. (See also the BT, Rosh Hashanah 36a.)

65. Most Jewish holidays come in the middle of the month, when the moon is full.

66. As mentioned in the sidebar "Days Of Hidden Aspect".

67. Cited by Rabbi Yehuda Dov Zinger in his book *Ziv Haminhagim*, pp. 150-51.

68. Zinger, ibid., p. 151.

69. Yalkut Shimoni, Part I, No. 95; taken from Rabbi Moshe Weissman, The Midrash Says: Beraishis (Genesis). Brooklyn, N.Y.: B'nei Ya'akov Pub., 1980, p. 44.

70. Gertrude Berg and Myra Waldo, The Molly Goldberg Jewish Cookbook. N.Y.: Pyramid Pub., 1977, p. 107.

CHESHVAN

1. Metzudat Tzion on that verse.

2. Rashi on the word "Bul."

3. Ki Tov, Vol. I, p. 250.

4. Radak, Rabbi David Kimchi (Rashi's grandson), on the words "B'yerech bul," (In the month of Bul.)

5. *I Kings* 12:25-13.

6. Ki Tov, ibid., p. 250.

7. Ki Tov, ibid., p. 251, quoting the Midrash Yalkut Shimoni, Kings 184.

8. Joan Nathan, The Jewish Holiday Kitchen. N.Y.: Schocken Books, 1979, p. 136.

9. "Potato," The World Book Encyclopedia, Chicago: Field Enterprises Educational Corp., 1970, Vol. 15, pp. 637-638.

10. From Tastefully Yours, Anne Schevelowitz, ed. N.Y.: Women's Organization of the Yeshiva High School of Queens; 1976; p. 40.

11. Eliyahu Ki Tov, Sefer HaToda'ah (Orig. Heb. Edition). Jerusalem: "A" Pub., 1971, part I, pp. 163-164.

12. *Jeremiah* 31:15-16.

13. Midrash quoted by Radak and Rashi, Jeremiah 31:14.
14. Ki Tov, BOH, Vol. I, pp. 257-258.
15. *Job* 1:5.
16. Ki Tov, ibid., p. 257.
17. From Judith Gethers and Elizabeth Lefft, <u>The World Famous Ratner's</u> <u>Meatless Cookbook</u>: U.S.A: Random House and Author's Pub., 1975 and 1991, p. 17.
18. Ibid., p. 19.
19. From Mildred G. Bellin, <u>The Original Jewish Cookbook</u>. N.Y.: Bloch Publishing Co., 1958 and 1983, p. 30.

KISLEV
1. Midrash Yalkut Melachim, 184.
2. Ki Tov, SeHaT, part I, p. 172.
3. Ki Tov, ibid., part I, p. 116.
4. Midrash Tanhuma, Tetsaveh, §6.
5. *Anaf Yosef* (commentary on the Midrash Tanhuma), Midrash Tanhuma, Tetsaveh, §6. This is the origin of the famous peace symbol of a dove carrying an olive branch.
6. Maimonides, MT, Book of Zmanim (Times), Laws of Hanukkah, 1:2.
7. Midrash Tanhuma, ibid.
8. ibid; Midrash Tanhuma, Tetsaveh, §8.
9. Midrash Tanhuma, Tetsaveh, §3.
10. Midrash Tanhuma, Tetsaveh, §6.
11. Midrash Rabbah, Tetsaveh, 36:1.
12. ibid.
13. Rashi on *Exodus* 27:20, "Constantly"; Nachmanides in Exodus, Chapter Tetsaveh; Rayvad (Rav Yosef David Kimchi) on the laws of Avodat Yom Kippur, Chapter 2 Halacha 2; Rashba's responsa Nos. 79 and 309; Tosfot Yom Tov on Mishnah Tamid 3:9.
14. Maimonides, MT, The Laws of Temidim and Musafim, 3:12.
15. BT, Shabbos 21b.
16. BT, Shabbos 22b.
17. Mishna Tamid 6:1.
18. Proverbs 20:27.
19. Midrash Tanhuma, Emor, §17; Midrash Rabah, Emor, §13.
20. Max L. Margolis and Alexander Marx, <u>A History of the Jewish People</u>. N.Y.: Harper and Row, 1965, pp. 130-141.
21. Nathan, ibid., p. 134.
22. Ki Tov, SeHaT, vol. 1, p. 171.
23. Midrash Ma'aseh Chanukah; Midrash L'Chanukah; Taken from J.D. Eisenstein, Editor, <u>Otzar HaMidrashim</u>, N.Y.: Joshua Eliyahu Grossman, 1956, Vol. 1, pp. 190, 192.
24. Ma'aseh Chanukah (2nd Manuscript), From J.D. Eisenstein, ibid., p. 190.

25. Ibid., p. 191.
26. BT, Gittin 57b; Eichah Rabbah 1:50; Pesikta Rabbasi 44:4; Seder Eliyahu
Rabbah chap. 30; Maccabees II chap. 7; Maccabees IV chap. 8-12; Josephus
chap. 19.
27. By Rabbi Yosef Bar Shlomo. See Otzar HaTefillos on Od'cha and Avodas
Yisrael, p. 637.
28. Retold from Josephus.
29. Gittin 57b.
30. *Psalms* 113:9.
31. Rabbi Nosson Scherman and Rabbi Meir Zlotowitz, Chanukah: Its History,
Observance and Significance. NY.; Mesorah Pub., 1981; 1990, pp. 70-77. This
section was apparently authored by Rabbi Hersh Goldwurm.
32. Midrash L'Chanukah; Ma'aseh Yehudit; Ma'aseh HaYehudit (All collected
from J.D. Eisenstein, Otsar Hamidrashim, vol. 1, "Chanukah," pp. 192-3,
"Judith," pp. 203-9); Book of Judith, Apocrypha; Ki Tov, SeHaT, part 1, p. 171)
33. Nathan, ibid., p. 134.

TEVET
1. Esther 9:31.
2. Ki Tov, BOH, vol. I, p. 323.
3. Ki Tov, ibid.
4. Louis I. Newman, The Hasidic Anthology: Tales and Teachings of the
Hasidim. Northvale, N.J: Jason Aronson, 1987, p. 112, No. 2.
5. Ki Tov, ibid., pp. 318-320. Taken from BT Megillah 9.
6. Ki Tov, ibid., p. 321.
7. Rashi, *Exodus* 34:35. Moses was emitting light in sharp rays or "horns", as if
the light were poking through a hole; see Habakuk 3:4 for a similar usage.
8. The Jew as devil started long before Michaelangelo. In John 8:44, Jews are
characterized as followers of the Devil. By the 13th century, it was not unusual
to see Jews portrayed with goat-like horns in dramatic performances. (Dov
Aharoni Fish, Jews For Nothing. NY.: Feldheim; pp. 39-40 and accompanying
footnotes.)
9. Ki Tov, ibid., p. 31.
10. Zinger, ibid., p. 265.
11. The sacrifices for Yom Kippur were taken directly from the Talmud, and
incorporated into the Yom Kippur prayer book; other ceremonies are listed in
the Mishnah and Talmud, some corroborated by non-Jewish sources.
12. Yearlings at Passover and Shavuot.
13. The quantities were: for Passover and Shavuot: two bulls, one ram and seven
lambs (all yearlings), every day; for Succot: thirteen young bulls, two rams, and
fourteen male lambs on the first day. The number of bulls decreased by one with
each successive day, until seven bulls were sacrificed on Shemini Azeret (the last
day of the festival).

14. See Tishrei: "The Water Libation".
15. For Passover and Shavuot: 3/10 of an ephah (1/10 of an ephah is the volume of 43.2 eggs) for each bull, 1/10 for each ram, and 1/10 for each lamb of the seven. (See Numbers 28:16-31.) For Succot: 3/10 of an ephah for the bulls, 2/10 of an ephah for the rams, and 1/10 of an ephah for the lambs. (See *Numbers* 29:12-39.)
16. Maimonides, MT, Laws of Fasts, 5:1.
17. See Nisan.
18. See Sivan.
19. Quoted from Maimonides, MT, Laws of the Pesach Sacrifice, 1:9.
20. See ShA OC §564 and accompanying MBs.
21. Ki Tov, ibid., vol. II, pp. 226-227.
22. Ki Tov, ibid., p. 239.
23. Ki Tov, Vol. I, p. 326. See the opening of Eichah Rabbah.

SHEVAT

1. Ki Tov, BOH, Vol. I, p. 346.
2. Mishnah Rosh Hashanah 1:1.
3. Ki Tov, ibid., pp. 347-348.
4. Ki Tov, ibid., p. 342.
5. Nachmanides, in his commentary to *Leviticus* 11:13, "These you shall detest from the birds..." and 17:11.
6. Rabbi Avrohom Chaim Feuer, "Fruit for the Soul," The Jewish Observer, January 1986, p. 10.
7. The Ari (Rabbi Yitzchak Luria), cited by Feuer, ibid.
8. Feuer, ibid.
9. Nachmanides, *Shaar Hagemul*, quoted in Feuer, p. 11.
10. BT, Megillah 6a.
11. BT, Berachos 44a. All of the information on the fruit of Israel and the Gennosar valley from: Feuer, ibid., pp. 9-11.
12. Rabbi Shlomo Yosef Zevin, The Festivals in Halacha. N.Y.: Mesorah Publications, Vol. II, pp. 124-127.
13. ShA OC 131:6.
14. Quoted in the MB No. 31 on the ShA, ibid.
15. MB, ibid.
16. Zinger, ibid., p. 268.
17. Zevin, ibid., p. 128.
18. Historical background courtesy of Zechariah Honikman, graduate student in Touro Graduate School of Jewish Studies. Suggested Source: Yichiel Michl Tukaatzinsky, *Sefer Eretz Yisroel*. Jerusalem: 1955, Heb.
19. David Geffen, "Uncommon Aspects of Tu B'Shevat," Jewish Digest. Jan. 1984, p. 63. Adapted from World Zionist Press Features.
20. Zevin, ibid.
21. Information from Z. Honikman.

22. Explained by Rabbi Shmuel Teich in a phone conversation.
23. Mr. Honikman would contend that these were actually *Mitnagdim* (literally: opposers), Torah authorities led by the Vilna Gaon who fought the Chasidic movement. (Their reasons are too complex to discuss here)
24. Explanation by Rabbi Teich.
25. This Tu B'Shevat Seder has four cups of wine, 15 different fruits, and 4 questions. The 4 questions are more specific forms of the ever-popular "Why is this day different from all other days?" Each question is discussed after one of the cups of wine.
26. *Sefer Hachinuch* Mitzvah 246.
27. BT, Tractate Rosh Hashanah, 9b.
28. Genesis 3:7.
29. BT, Tractate Berachot, 57a.
30. "Vine" here refers to a grape vine.
31. "Fig," Teutsch and Frankel, The Encyclopedia of Jewish Symbols. p. 53.
32. The date is praised for its nourishment in BT, Berachot 12a.
33. Judges 4:5.
34. JT, Bikkurim 1:3.
35. Genesis Rabbah 41:1.
36. Numbers Rabbah 3:1.
37. Deuteronomy 34:3; Judges 1:16; Judges 3:13; II Chronicles 28:15.

ADAR

1. BT, Ta'anit 29a.
2. Ibid.
3. Exodus 17:7.
4. Rashi on Exodus 17:8. This does not necessarily mean that Amalek consciously waited to attack until we had sinned; they probably had no idea what was happening.
5. Me'am Loez, commentator on Esther 1:5, quoted by the Artscroll Megillah, p. 43.
6. Yalkut Shimoni
7. Pirchei L'vanon, quoted in the Artscroll Megillah.
8. BT, Shabbat 88a.
9. The *S'fas Emes*, quoted by the Artscroll Megillah, p. 130.
10. From Jennie Grossinger, The Art of Jewish Cooking. N.Y.: Random House, Inc.; 1958; pp. 39-40.
11. Esther 4:16.
12. Zinger, ibid., pp. 274-275.
13. Maimonides, MT, The Book of Zemanim, Laws of Megillah 2:15; BT, Pesachim, 109a.

14. Ki Tov, BOH, ibid., Vol. II, pp. 84, 86.
15. Ki Tov, ibid., Vol. II, p. 85.
16. Ohel Ya'akov, Chapter on Re'ei, from Avraham Kriv, <u>Shabbat U'moed Bidrush Ub'chasidut</u>. Tel Aviv: Dvir Pub., 1966, pp. 374-375. Heb.
17. *Leviticus* 23:28.
18. Ki Tov, ibid., pp. 86-87.
19. Nathan, ibid., pp. 160, 164.
20. Nathan, ibid., p. 164.
21. The *Yabia Omer*, cited by Avraham Kriv in <u>*Shabbat Umoed Bidrush Ub'Chasidut*</u>, ibid., pp. 386-387.
22. BT, Megillah, 7b.
23. Mostly paraphrased from <u>The Hasidic Anthology</u>, ibid., 141:5, p. 361.
24. Ki Tov, BOH, ibid., Vol. II, pp. 85, 87-88.
25. Ki Tov, ibid., Vol. II, pp. 88-89.
26. Ki Tov, SeHaT, ibid., part I, p. 180.
27. Rabbi Judah Leib Graubart, "*Yabia Omer*," quoted in Avraham Kriv, <u>*Shabbat Umoed Bidrush Ub'Chasidut*</u>, ibid., p. 387.
28. Zinger, ibid., p. 280.
29. Cited in the name of the Chafetz Chaim by Rabbi Zinger, <u>Ziv Haminhagim</u>, ibid.
30. Ki Tov, BOH, ibid., Vol. II, p. 94.
31. "And all who send more to their friends are praised." From ShA OC §595, No.4.
32. MB No. 20 on ShA OC §596.
33. From a conversation with Rabbi Yehoshua Leiman.

<u>LEAP MONTH: ADAR ALEPH/BET</u>
1. Ki Tov, SeHaT, Part I, p. 197.
2. This imperative is derived from a verse in Deuteronomy 16:1: "Preserve the month of Spring and keep the Passover unto the Lord thy God."
3. Midrash Rabbah on Exodus 15:3; also Exodus Rabbah Nos. 15-24.
4. Nachmanides, Sefer HaZakhuth, on Rif Gittin 34b; Nachmanides Aderes Harishonim vol. III, (1967 edition: Volume V), Pages 375-376; Tzemach David 4118; Seder Hadorot 4118.
5. JT, Pesachim 4:9.
6. Rabbi Zechariah Fendel, <u>Legacy of Sinai: A History of Torah Transmission with World Backgrounds</u>, N.Y.: Rabbi Jacob Joseph School Press, 1981, p. 202 and footnotes 89-91.
7. Aderes Harishonim, Vol. III, p. 376. All of this material cited by Rabbi Fendel on p. 202.
8. BT, Sanhedrin 42a.
9. BT, Sanhedrin 12a. I have taken the English translation of the coded text from <u>A History of the Jewish People</u>, Vol. I: From Yavneh to Pumbedisa. N.Y.: Mesorah Pub., 1986, p. 185.

10. Rabbeinu Nasson ben Reb Yechiel Gaon, born in 1010 C.E.

11. Referred to here as "offspring of Nachshon" because Nachshon was the first Nasi mentioned in the Torah.

12. Nitsiv refers to the officials under King Solomon for each month of the year. See *I Kings* 4:7.

13. Rome has become synonymous with Edom.

14. The sages of the Sanhedrin were referred to as the Masters of Gatherings; one example is found in the Targum, *Ecclesiastes* 12:11.

15. The sages of the Sanhedrin had to decide on the leap year in Av, eight months early. The court convened when it could at this point; there was no guarantee they could make that decision in Adar, so they made it in Av.

16. From Barbara Schultz, "There's a Hungarian in Your Kitchen!", Jewish Sentinel. Feb. 3-9, 1995, p. 20.

17. From North Shore Hebrew Academy Cookbook

18. "Hydroponics," *Encyclopedia Yisroelit*, pp. 123-127.

19. "Hydroponics," Columbia Encyclopedia.

20. "Hydroponics," *Encyclopedia Yisroelit*, ibid.

21. Mindy Hermann, "Soy Healthy." American Health. July/August 1992, p. 88.

NISAN

1. Ki Tov, BOH, ibid., Vol. II, pp. 127, 130-131.

2. Ki Tov, ibid., pp. 117-118.

3. Ki Tov, ibid., pp. 129-130.

4. Nachmanides, *Exodus* 12:2.

5. Nachmanides, Ibid.

6. Ki Tov, SeHaT, ibid., part II, p. 10.

7. Ki Tov, BOH, ibid., pp.124-127.

8. Ki Tov, ibid., p. 129.

9. See Tishrei: The Prayer for Rain.

10. Ki Tov, BOH, ibid., Vol. II, pp. 352-353.

11. Ki Tov, ibid., pp. 370-371.

12. Ki Tov, ibid.

13. My thanks to Rabbi Yehoshua Leiman, for this cogent explanation.

14. Zevin, ibid., p. 75.

15. *Deuteronomy* 26:8; cited in Haggadah.

16. Zevin, ibid., vol. III, pp. 77-78, 80-83, and Nathan, ibid., p. 180.

17. MB No. 4 on ShA OC 455:1.

18. Ki Tov, BOH, ibid., pp. 193-195.

19. Ki Tov, ibid., p. 194.

20. M. Glazerson, The Secrets of the Haggadah. Jerusalem: Raz Ot Inst., 1989, p. 48.

21. Ki Tov, ibid., p. 193.

22. Ki Tov, ibid.

23. Zevin, ibid., Vol. III, pp. 26-28, citing Exodus 12:4.

24. Zevin, ibid., p. 131.
25. Rabbi Chaim Preiss, What is the Reason?. N.Y.: Bloch Publishing Company, 1976, vol. 6: Pesach, p. 69.
26. Glazerson, ibid., p. 38.
27. From M. Glazerson, ibid.
28. Preiss, ibid., p. 74.
29. Ki Tov, ibid., p. 285.
30. Teutsch and Frankel, The Encyclopedia of Jewish Symbols, p. 46.
31. Preiss, ibid., p. 75.
32. Ki Tov, ibid., p. 285.
33. Glazerson, ibid., pp. 30-31.
34. Nathan, ibid., p. 176.
35. Ki Tov, ibid., pp. 281-282.
36. Rabbi Solomon Ganzfried, Code of Jewish Law. N.Y.: Hebrew Pub. Company, 1963, vol. III, p. 46. Hyman E. Goldin, LL.B., Tr.
37. Ki Tov, ibid., pp. 280-281.
38. From Rabbi Avrohom Blumenkrantz, The Laws of Pesach: A Digest. N.J.: Gross Bros. Printing Co., 1995, p.26-2.
39. Rav Yizchak Sender, The Commentator's Haggadah. Spring Valley, N.Y.: Feldheim Publishers Inc., 1991, p. 14.
40. Mishnah Kidushin, 1:7.
41. BT, Pesachim 108a.
42. Ki Tov, ibid., p. 270.
43. Nachmanides Exodus 1:11.
44. Rashi, Exodus 1:16.
45. Nehama Leibowitz, Studies in Exodus. Jerusalem: World Zionist Organization, 1981, pp. 31-35, 37-38, note 8. This is part of her major work, a series examining, in the most delightful and thought-provoking way, each book of the Pentateuch.
46. Rashi, *Exodus* 1:15; Sotah 11b.
47. Ibn Ezra, *Exodus* 1:15; Or HaChayim, ibid.
48. Rashi, *Exodus* 38:8.
49. Rashi, ibid.
50. Sotah 12a.
51. Midrash Exodus Rabbah 1:12; BT, Sotah 11b.
52. Midrash Exodus Rabbah, 1:22.
53. Midrash *Proverbs* 14:1.
54. Ki Tov, ibid., pp. 161-162.

IYAR
1. Ki Tov, BOH, ibid., Vol. III, p. 15.
2. Ki Tov, SeHaT, ibid., part II, p. 251.
3. Nachmanides, *Exodus* 16:1 and 16:4.

4. Rashi *Exodus* 16:1.
5. Rashi, ibid.
6. Rashi, *Exodus* 16:14.
7. Zevin, <u>The Festivals in Halacha</u>. N.Y.: Mesorah Pub., 1982, p. 217.
8. Ben Isaiah, Linear translation, *Exodus* 16:15.
9. Rashi, ibid.
10. *Exodus* 16:14.
11. Rashi, *Exodus* 16:4.
12. *Exodus* 16:16.
13. Rashi, *Exodus* 16:17.
14. *Exodus* 16:19.
15. BT, Yuma 75a.
16. Rashi, *Numbers* 11:8.
17. BT, Yuma 75b.
18. *Exodus* 16:20.
19. Harry Thomas Frank, <u>Discovering the Biblical World</u>. James F. Strange, editor. Maplewood, N.J.: Hammond Inc., 1988, p. 59.
20. Everyone is obligated to have two loaves of Challah (Lechem Mishnah) at their Shabbat meal. (See ShA OC 274:1.)
21. Freda Reider, <u>The Hallah Book: Recipes, History, and Traditions</u>. N.Y.: Ktav Publications, 1987, p. 6.
22. *Exodus* 17; *Numbers* 11:4.
23. *Exodus* 12:38.
24. Reider, ibid., pp. 5-8; also ShA OC 300:1.
25. Reider, ibid.
26. Custom known by Mordechai Housman.
27. *Numbers* 32:1.
28. *Numbers* 11: 31.
29. Rashi, *Numbers* 11:4.
30. *Numbers* 11:4.
31. *Numbers* 11:32-3.
32. Rashi, *Numbers* 11:4.
33. Ki Tov, BOH, ibid., Vol. III, pp. 31-32.
34. Zinger, ibid. p. 104.
35. Ki Tov, ibid.
36. BT, Yevamot p. 62.
37. Ki Tov, ibid., Vol.II, p. 404.
38. Ki Tov, ibid., Vol. III, pp. 36-37.
39. Zevin, ibid., p. 202.
40. See Tishrei and Nisan.
41. Ki Tov, ibid., Vol. II, p. 363.
42. Rabbi Ki Tov cites this ancient Kabbalistic tradition. (Ki Tov, ibid., Vol. III, p. 37.

43. Zevin, ibid., Vol. III, p. 218.
44. Zinger, ibid., p. 104.
45. Zevin, ibid., Vol. III, pp. 224-225.
46. Zevin, ibid., Vol. III, p. 221.
47. Chatam Sofer, responsa, Yoreh De'ah, 233. Quoted in Rabbi Shlomo Yosef Zevin, ibid., Vol. III, p. 222.
48. From Sho'el UMeshiv, fifth edition, §39. Quoted in Zevin, Vol. III, pp. 222-223.
49. Zevin, ibid., Vol. III, p. 226.

SIVAN
1. Ramah (Rabbi Moshe Iserlis), commentary on ShA OC 494:3.
2. *Exodus* 19:8; 24:3; 24:7; Numbers 32:31.
3. BT, Shabbat 88a.
4. Nathan, ibid., p. 130.
5. *Exodus* 4:31.
6. *Exodus* 24:7.
7. *Genesis* 3:7.
8. "Apple," Man, Myth and Magic: An Illustrated Encyclopedia of the Supernatural. Richard Cavendish, Ed. N.Y.: Marshall Cavendish Corp., 1970, pp. 109-110.
9. From Aryeh Kaplan's "Waters of Eden," in The Aryeh Kaplan Anthology Vol II, N.Y.: NCSY/OU. 1974, p. 373.
10. N. Ts. Gotlib, Amudai Torah. Jerusalem: Machon Gachelet, 1989, Vol. 1, p. 251. Heb.
11. BT, Ketuboth, 62b.
12. *Deuteronomy* 33:2.
13. *Isaiah* 55:1.
14. *Genesis* 3:24.
15. BT, Ta'anit 7a.
16. *V'samachta Bechagecha*, mentioned in Deuteronomy 16:14.
17. ShA OC §494.
18. A commentary by the Chafetz Chaim, a 19th Century authority.
19. Eliyahu Ki Tov refers to this in the name of Rabbi Shimshon of Ostropol (Ki Tov, BOH, ibid., Vol. III, p. 73.)
20. From a phone conversation with Mordechai Housman, a Hassidic friend, who has seen this custom practiced.
21. Nathan, ibid., p. 214.
22. Ki Tov, BOH, ibid., Vol. III, p. 72.
23. Ki Tov, ibid., p. 73.

TAMMUZ
1. Based on Zechariah 8:19.
2. Ibid.

3. See Mishnah there; also, Mishnah Ta'anit 4:1.
4. Rabbi Yehuda Dov Zinger, ibid., p. 120. The Torah records this incident in Exodus 32:19.
5. Nachmanides on Exodus 32:19.
6. Rashi on same.
7. Zinger, ibid.
8. Zinger, ibid., p. 121.
9. Ki Tov, BOH, ibid., Vol. III, pp. 203-204.
10. JT, cited by Zinger, ibid., p. 121.
11. ibid.
12. *Lamentations* 1:3.

AV
1. Commentary of *Kuntrus Acharon* of Rabbi Avraham Yitzchak Sperling's Ta'amei Haminhagim Umikorei Hadinim. Jerusalem: Eshkol Publishing, 1972, p. 285. Heb.
2. Zinger, ibid., p. 130; Ki Tov, BOH, ibid., Vol. III, pp. 211-212.
3. *Psalms* 137: 5-7.
4. ShA OC §552, 1, and accompanying MB passages.
5. Zinger, ibid., p. 132.
6. MB No. 5 on ShA OC §552.
7. Ki Tov, ibid., Vol. III, p. 212.
8. Ki Tov, ibid., p. 214.
9. Ki Tov, ibid., p. 245.
10. *Exodus* 25:8.
11. Zinger, ibid., p. 121.
12. BT, Gittin 57a; JT, Ta'anit 4:5.
13. Zinger, ibid., p. 122.
14. ShA OC 552:4.
15. From Be'eir Heitev commentary #5 on ShA OC 552:4.
16. ShA OC 552:3, and accompanying MB passages.
17. ShA OC 552:3.
18. MB No. 9 on ShA OC ibid.
19. Suggested by Mordechai Housman.
20. Ramah (Rabbi Moshe Iserlis), commenting on the ShA OC 552:9.
21. ShA OC 552:7.
22. Rabbi Avrohom Chaim Feuer and Rabbi Avie Gold, The Complete Tisha B'av Service. N.Y.: Mesorah Pub., 1991, p. 469.
23. ShA OC 552:5.
24. Zinger, ibid., p. 132.
25. *Genesis* 25:29-34.
26. The oval shape helps distribute the force applied to the egg.

27. Rabbi Avrohom Katz, <u>Designer World</u>. England: GJBS, 1994, pp. 174-175.
28. Katz, ibid., pp. 172-178.

ELUL
1. Ki Tov, ibid., Vol. III, p. 319.
2. Ki Tov, ibid., Vol. III, pp. 319-320.
3. Ki Tov, ibid., Vol. III, p. 321.
4. Ki Tov, ibid., Vol. III, p. 320.
5. Maimonides, MT, Laws of Teshuvah 3:4; quoted in Ki Tov, ibid., Vol. I, p. 31.
6. Translation by Rabbi A.J. Rosenberg in <u>The Book of Twelve Prophets</u>. N.Y.: The Judaica Press, 1986, p. 127.
7. Artscroll Machzor, Rosh Hashanah, ibid., p. 483.
8. BT, Rosh Hashanah 16b.
9. Heard in a tape from a series of lectures given by Rabbi Noach Weinberg, the Rosh Yeshiva of Aishet Torah.
10. Ibid.
11. Much of this material was culled from the entries in <u>Sefer Hachinuch</u> on the laws of different sacrifices, and from Maimonides' MT, Book of Service(Avodah), Laws of Ma'asei Hakorbanot (Sacrifices), Chap. 3.
12. Quoted by the Me'am Loez on Pirkei Avot 5:5.
13. In fact, the Messiah is supposed to come from David's line.
14. Teutsch and Frankel, "Salt," <u>The Encyclopedia of Jewish Symbols</u>, pp. 142-3.
15. Rav Aharon Halevi, <u>*Sefer Hachinuch*</u>. Jerusalem: Eshkol Pub., 1958, p. 59, Nos. 118, 119.
16. *Leviticus* 2:13.
17. Teutsch and Frankel, Ibid.
18. Rashi, *Leviticus* 2:13, "Covenant of Salt". Based on Midrashic sources.
19. Nachmanides, quoted in <u>The Chumash: Stone Edition</u>. Rabbi Nosson Scherman, Ed. N.Y.: Mesorah Pub., 1993., p. 553.
20. Rav Aharon Halevi, <u>*Sefer Hachinuch*</u>, ibid., No. 119.
21. ibid.
22. Rabbi Moshe Iserlis on the ShA Orach Chayim, Hilchot B'tziyat Hapat, 167:5.
23. ShA OC 167:5 and commentary by the Ramah (Rabbi Moshe Iserlis.)
24. ShA OC 167:5.
25. Magen Avraham
26. MB No. 32 on Rabbi Moshe Iserlis, ShA OC 167:5.
27. ShA OC 167:4.
28. Maimonides, MT, Book of Service (Avodah), Hilchot Ma'asei Hakorbanot, 3:6; 3:8; 3:10; 3:14-15.
29. MB No. 23 on ShA OC 167:4.
30. Mordechai Housman gave me the lead on this; while it is listed in the ShA, I have not been able to find the place.

RECIPE REFERENCE

Here are some additional simple recipes to enjoy. Please refer to months of Tishrei & Kislev for basic Kosher cookbook references.

TISHREI

"Fluffy Honey Cake," The Haimishe Kitchen Vol. II. Compiled and Ed. by the Ladies Auxiliary of Nitra. Mt. Kisco, N.Y.: 1985, p. 189.

"Raisin Challah," Spice and Spirit: The Complete Kosher Jewish Cookbook. N.Y.: Lubavitch Women's Cookbook Pub. & Bookmart Press, 1990, p. 53.

"September — Apple Cholent," Kay Kantor Pomerantz, Come For Cholent... Again! N.Y.: Bloch Publishing, 1994, p. 30.

KISLEV

"Traditional Potato Latkes," Sara Finkel, Classic Kosher Cooking. Michigan: Targum-Feldheim, 1989, p. 164.

"Zucchini Pancakes," New Kosher Cuisine For All Seasons. Ivy Feuerstadt and Melinda Strauss. Berkeley, CA.: Ten Speed Press, 1993, p. 69.

"December — Latke Cholent," Come For Cholent... Again!, p. 33.

"Israeli Style Sufganiyot," New Kosher Cuisine For All Seasons, p. 73.

TEVET

Simple Foods:

"Macaroni & Cheese Casserole," Spice and Spirit, p. 96.

"Classic Dinner Rice," ibid., p. 316.

Breaking the Fast:

"October — Break the Fast Cholent!", Come For Cholent... Again!, p. 31.

SHEVAT

"Bible Fruit Salad," New Kosher Cuisine For All Seasons, pp. 142-143.

"Fruit Cup," Spice and Spirit, p. 460.

ADAR

"Broiled Chicken with Wine and Mushrooms," Classic Kosher Cooking, p. 83.

"Bourbon Chicken," New Kosher Cuisine For All Seasons, p. 199.

"Homemade Wine," The Taste of Shabbos: The Complete Sabbath Cookbook. Editorial Committee: Dvorah Eisenbach, Zelda Goldfield, Shifra Slater. N.Y.: Feldheim Publishers, A Project of Aish Hatorah Women's Organization, 1988, pp. 9-11.

"Sweet Gefilte Fish," ibid., p. 16.

"Basic Fried Flounder, Spice and Spirit, p. 160.

ADAR BEIT

"Tofu Lasagna", Spice and Spirit, p. 97.

"Gemuse Soup (Vegetable Soup)," Rose Friedman, Jewish Vegetarian Cooking. Northampton, England: HarperCollins Publishers, 1984; 1992, p. 37.

NISAN
"Homemade Horseradish," Spice and Spirit, p. 338.
"Tuna-Horseradish Dip," New Kosher Cuisine For All Seasons, p. 136.
(Note: The horseradish at the Passover Seder is simply grated horseradish root.)
"Orange Charoset," Classic Kosher Cooking, p. 277.
"Matzo Kleis (Matzo Meal Soup Dumplings)," Jewish Vegetarian Cooking, p. 154.
"Pareve Matzoh Kugel," New Kosher Cuisine For All Seasons, p. 119.

IYAR
"Chicken Soup," New Kosher Cuisine For All Seasons, p. 7.
"Classic Challah," Spice and Spirit, p. 51.
"Sweet Half-and-Half Challah," The Taste of Shabbos: The Complete Sabbath Cookbook, pp. 3-4.
"Four-Strand Braided Challah," ibid., p. 5.
"Matzoh Brei," Spice and Spirit, p. 79.

SIVAN
"Refreshing Summer Gazpacho," Classic Kosher Cooking, p. 72.
"Old Fashioned Cheesecake," The Haimishe Kitchen Vol. II, p. 212.
"Cheese Blintze Supreme," The Taste of Shabbos: The Complete Sabbath Cookbook, p. 140.
"Tsavay (Yogurt or Sour Cream With Vegetables)," Jewish Vegetarian Cooking, p. 31.

AV
"Egg Salad," Spice and Spirit, p. 79.
"Eier Mit Tzibbale I (Egg and Onion)," Jewish Vegetarian Cooking, p. 28.
"Sephardic Cholent," Spice and Spirit, p. 209.
(Includes chickpeas, curry, meat, potatoes, and hard-boiled eggs.)
"Lentil Salad," Jewish Vegetarian Cooking, p. 116.

ELUL
"Potted Veal Roast," Classic Kosher Cooking, p. 104.
"Roast Beef," ibid., p. 101.
"Schnitzel," ibid., p. 84.

These sources are helpful for those interested in learning more about Kashruth and keeping a Kosher home:
Spice and Spirit, pp. 15-38. (See Tishrei) This covers all the food groups, and their kosher requirements. All about the kosher kitchen, written in a friendly, straightforward way.

Rabbi Yacov Lipschutz, Kashruth. N.Y.: Mesorah Pub., 1988, pp. 96-137. For information on kosher cooking and baking, esp. a section on additives used in packaged foods, plus explanations of kashruth problems.

BIBLIOGRAPHY

PRIMARY TORAH SOURCES:

Commentaries, such as Rashi and Nachmanides, on Torah passages cited.

Babylonian Talmud, segments from Tractates Hullin, Rosh Hashanah, Sukah, Ketuboth, Kiddushin, Sanhedrin, Shabbos, Sotah, Gittin, Megillah, Berachot, Ta'anit, Pesachim, Yevamot, and Yuma.

Jerusalem Talmud, segments from Tractates Sukah, Bikkurim, Pesachim, & Ta'anit.

Midrashim in Pirkei De Rabbi Eliezer, Midrash Rabbah, Midrash Tanhuma, Midrash Yalkut Melachim, Midrash Konen, Yalkut Shimoni, and Midrash Proverbs; Various Midrashim on Chanukah and Judith quoted in the Otzar Midrashim (See citation below).

Sources in Mishnah Rosh Hashanah, Tamid, Ta'anit and Kiddushin.

Maimonides' Mishnah Torah, sections in Laws of Teshuvah; Prayer; Hannukah; Temidim and Musafim; Fasts; The Pesach Sacrifice; Megillah; and Ma'asei Hakorbanot (Sacrifices).

Mishnah Brurah and Shulchan Aruch, sections cited.

OTHER SOURCES

Agus, Arlene, "This Month is for You: Observing Rosh Hodesh as a Woman's Holiday," Elizabeth Koltun, Jewish Women, New Perspectives. N.Y.: Schocken Publishers, 1986, pp. 84-93.

"Apple," Man, Myth and Magic: An Illustrated Encyclopedia of the Supernatural. Richard Cavendish, Ed. N.Y.: Marshall Cavendish Corp., 1970, pp. 109-110.

The Artscroll Megillah. Tr. and comp. by Rabbi Meir Zlotowitz. N.Y.: ArtScroll Studios Press, 1976.

Fish, Dov Aharoni , Jews For Nothing. N.Y.: Feldheim.

The Artscroll Tehillim (Psalms), tr. and annot. by Rabbi Hillel Danziger with Rabbi Nosson Scherman. N.Y.: Mesorah Pub., 1988.

The Complete Artscroll Machzor, Rosh Hashanah ed., Nusach Ashkenaz. Rabbi Nosson Scherman, Tr. and Rabbi Meir Zlotowitz, Co-ed. N.Y.: Mesorah Pub., 1985.

The Complete Artscroll Siddur. Rabbi Nosson Scherman and Rabbi Meir Zlotowitz, Eds. N.Y.: Mesorah Pub., 1985; 1989; 1992.

The Chumash: Stone Edition. Rabbi Nosson Scherman, Ed., N.Y.: Mesorah Pub., 1993.

Eisenstein, J.D., Ed., Otzar HaMidrashim, N.Y.: Joshua Eliyahu Grossman, 1956, Vol. 1.

Fendel, Rabbi Zechariah, Legacy of Sinai: A History of Torah Transmission with World Backgrounds. N.Y.: Rabbi Jacob Joseph School Press, 1981, p. 202 and footnotes 89-91.

Frank, Harry Thomas, Discovering the Biblical World. James F. Strange, Ed. Maplewood, N.J.: Hammond, Inc., 1988.

Feuer, Rabbi Avrohom Chaim, "Fruit for the Soul," The Jewish Observer, Jan. 1986, pp. 9-12.

Feuer, Rabbi Avrohom Chaim and Gold, Rabbi Avie, The Complete Tisha B'av Service. N.Y.: Mesorah Pub., 1991.

"Food," Encyclopedia Judaica, Vol. 9.

Ganzfried, Rabbi Solomon, <u>Code of Jewish Law</u>. N.Y.: Hebrew Publishing. 1963, vol. III. Hyman E. Goldin, Tr.

Geffen, David, "Uncommon Aspects of Tu B'Shevat," <u>Jewish Digest</u>. Jan. 1984, pp. 63-64.

Glazerson, M., <u>The Secrets of the Haggadah</u>. Jerusalem: Raz Ot Institute, 1989.

Gotlib, N. Ts., <u>Amudai Torah</u>. Jerusalem: Machon Gachelet, 1989, Vol. I, pp. 250-253. Heb.

Halevi, Rav Aharon, *Sefer Hachinuch*. Jerusalem: Eshkol Pub., 1958.

<u>A History of the Jewish People</u>, Vol. I: From Yavneh to Pumbedisa. N.Y.: Mesorah Pub., 1986, p. 185.

"Hydroponics," <u>Columbia Encyclopedia</u> and in Encyclopedia Yisroelit.

<u>The Jerusalem Bible: The Holy Scriptures</u>. Jerusalem: Koren Pub., 1989.

Kahati, Pinchas, <u>Kahati Edition, Mishnah Seder Mo'ed, Rosh Hashanah</u> 1:2. Jerusalem: Haichal Shlomo, 1992.

Kaplan, Aryeh, "Waters of Eden," <u>The Aryeh Kaplan Anthology Vol. II</u>, N.Y.: NCSY/OU, 1974, pp. 372-377.

Katz, Rabbi Avrohom, <u>Designer World</u>. England: GJBS, 1994.

Ki Tov, Eliyahu, *Sefer Hatoda'ah* (Heb.) Jerusalem: "A" Pub., 1971, parts 1-2.

Ki Tov, Eliyahu, <u>The Book Of Our Heritage</u>. Tr. from Heb. Sefer Hatoda'ah by Nathan Bulman. N.Y.: Feldheim Publishers, 1978, Vol. 1-3.

Kriv, Avraham, *Shabbat U'moed Bidrush Ub'chasidut*. (Heb.) Tel Aviv: Dvir Pub., 1966.

Leibowitz, Nehama, <u>Studies in Exodus</u>. Jerusalem: World Zionist Org., 1981, pp. 31-35, 37-38, note 8.

Margolis, Max L. and Marx, Alexander, <u>A History of the Jewish People</u>. N.Y.: Harper and Row, 1965.

Nathan, Joan, <u>The Jewish Holiday Kitchen</u>. N.Y.: Schocken Books, 1979.

Newman, Louis I., <u>The Hasidic Anthology: Tales and Teachings of the Hasidim</u>. Northvale, N.J.: Jason Aronson, 1987.

Nussbaum, Rabbi Chaim, <u>The Essence of Teshuvah: A Path to Repentance</u>. Northvale, N.J.: Jason Aronson, 1993.

"Potato," <u>The World Book Encyclopedia</u>, Chicago: Field Enterprises Educational Corp., 1970, Vol. 15, pp. 637-638.

Preiss, Rabbi Chaim, <u>What is the Reason?</u> N.Y.: Bloch Publishing Company, 1976, vol. 6: Pesach.

Premisla, Rabbi Moses of, <u>Mateh Moshe</u>. Jerusalem: 1984, Part 5.

Reider, Freda, <u>The Hallah Book: Recipes, History, and Traditions.</u> N.Y.: Ktav Publications, 1987.

Rosenberg, Rabbi A.J., <u>The Book of the Twelve Prophets, Vol. Two</u>. N.Y.: Judaica Press, 1988.

Rabbi Nosson Scherman and Rabbi Meir Zlotowitz, <u>Chanukah: Its History, Observance and Significance</u>. N.Y.: Mesorah Pub., 1981; 1990.

<u>Sefer Hemdat Hayamim</u>, Vol. 1, p. 25.

Sender, Rav Yitzchak, <u>The Commentator's Haggadah</u>. Spring Valley, N.Y.: Feldheim Publishers Inc., 1991, p. 14.

Soloveitchik, Rabbi Joseph Dov, <u>On Repentance</u>. Jerusalem: World Zionist Org., 1975.

Sperling, Rabbi Avraham Yitzchak, *Ta'amei Haminhagim Umikorei Hadinim*. Jerusalem: Eshkol Publishing, 1972.

Teutsch and Frankel, The Encyclopedia of Jewish Symbols. pp. 46, 53, 142-143.

Weissman, Rabbi Moshe, The Midrash Says: Beraishis (Genesis). Brooklyn, N.Y.: B'nei Ya'akov Pub., 1980.

Zevin, Rabbi Shlomo Yosef, The Festivals In Halacha. N.Y.: Mesorah Pub., V. I-III.

Zinger, Rabbi Yehudah Dov, *Ziv Haminhagim* (Heb.) Jerusalem: Dror Pub., 1971.

Zuckerman Matitya, Rivka and Sobel, Ilana, "Tu B'Shvat Seder," From Internet: Gopher Jerusalem1.datasrv.col.il/ Special Tu B'Shvat Holiday Section/ Tu B'Shvat From the WZO Student Department/ Program Ideas/ Tu B'Shvat Seder.

COOKBOOKS (See also Recipe Reference):

Bellin, Mildred B., The Original Jewish Cookbook. N.Y.: Bloch Pub., 1958, 1983.

Berg, Gertrude and Waldo, Myra, The Molly Goldberg Jewish Cookbook. N.Y.: Pyramid Pub., 1977.

Blumenkrantz, Rabbi Avrohom, The Laws of Pesach: A Digest. N.J.: Gross Bros. Printing Co., 1995.

Finkel, Sara, Classic Kosher Cooking. (See Kislev here)

Friedman, Rose, Jewish Vegetarian Cooking. (See Adar Beit here)

Gethers, Judith and Lefft, Elizabeth, The World Famous Ratner's Meatless Cookbook. U.S.A.: Random House and Author's Pub., 1975 and 1991.

Grossinger, Jennie, The Art of Jewish Cooking. N.Y.: Random House, 1958.

The Haimishe Kitchen Vol. II. Compiled and Ed. by the Ladies Auxiliary of Nitra. Mt. Kisco, N.Y.: 1985.

Lipschutz, Rabbi Yacov, Kashruth. N.Y.: Mesorah Pub., 1988, pp. 96-137.

North Shore Hebrew Academy Cookbook

Pomerantz, Kay Kantor, Come For Cholent...Again! N.Y.: Bloch Publishing, 1994.

Schevelowitz, Anne, Ed., Tastefully Yours. N.Y.: Women's Org. of the Yeshiva H.S. of Queens, 1976.

Schultz, Barbara, "There's a Hungarian in Your Kitchen!", Jewish Sentinel. Feb. 3-9, 1995, p. 20.

Spice and Spirit: The Complete Kosher Jewish Cookbook. N.Y.: Lubavitch Women's Cookbook Pub. & Bookmart Press, 1990.

The Taste of Shabbos: The Complete Sabbath Cookbook. Editorial Committee: Dvorah Eisenbach, Zelda Goldfield, Shifra Slater. N.Y.: Feldheim Publishers, A Project of Aish Hatorah Women's Organization, 1988.

Wasserman, Debra. The Lowfat Jewish Vegetarian Cookbook, Vegetarian Resource Group, POB 1463, Baltimore, MD., 21203,

FURTHER READING

ON ROSH HODESH*
Helfgott, Esther Altshul, "Rosh Chodesh: The New Moon," The Jewish Observer, Jan. 30, 1987.
Schor, Binah, "Rosh Chodesh: Back to the Sources I: Midrash," Neshama,** Winter 1992, Vol. 4 No. 4, p. 9.
ON FOODS
Brower, Vicki, "I Saw the Lite: Biblical Food was a Wholesome Mix of Sophisticated Cuisines," American Health, Vol. 9, Dec. 1990, p. 88.
Cohen, Jayne, "Rosh Hashanah: Culinary Customs From Around the World," Gourmet, Vol. 53, Sept. 1993, pp. 116-117.
de Silva, Cara, "Nectar of the New Year," New York Newsday, Wed., Aug. 31, 1994, pp. B25-B26.
Freudenstein, Eric G., "Eating Fish ('Gefilte' and Other) on Shabbat," Jewish Digest, Dec. 1980, pp. 65-71. Condensed from Judaism Vol. 29 No. 4.
Kayte, Lillian, "Celebrating Rosh Hashanah," Vegetarian Times, Sept. 1993, p. 58.
Lipman, K.I., "A Delicate Twist On Classic Challah," Sunset (Central West Ed.), Vol. 191, Sept. 1993, p. 106.
Sliw, Yitzchok, "Meat: The Issues: An Analysis of Vegetarianism in the Light of Biblical, Talmudic and Rabbinic Teachings," L'Eylah, London, 9/93, V. 36, pp. 25-29.
Sheraton, Mimi, "A Jewish Yen for Chinese," The New York Times Magazine, Vol. 140, Sept. 23, 1990, p. 71 Col. 1.
Waldman, Nahum M., "Food Symbolism in Jewish Life," Midstream, Summer, 1989, p. 23-24.
White, Susan J., "Vegetables of the Bible," The Paper Pomegranate, Summer 1993, Vol. XVII No. 1, p. 7.
BOOKS ON FOOD
Anderson, Alexander Walter, Plants of the Bible. N.Y.: Philosophical Library, 1957.
Angel, Gilda, Sephardic Holiday Cooking. Decalogue Books, Mount Vernon, N.Y., 1986.
Cooper, John, Eat and Be Satisfied: A Social History of Jewish Food. Northvale, N.J.: Jason Aronson, 1993.
Liebman, Malina W., Jewish Cookery: From Boston to Baghdad. N.Y.: Nightingale Resource Books, 1989.
Locke, Norton, The Land of Milk and Honey. Fort Lauderdale, FL.: Ashley Pub., 1992.
Moldenke, Harold Norman, Plants of the Bible. Ronald Press Co., 1952.
Murray, Michael T., M.D., The Healing Power of Herbs. Rocklin, CA.: Prima Pub., 1992.
Rabinowitz, Louis I., Torah and Flora. N.Y.: Sanhedrin Press, 1977.
Stavroulakis, Nicholas, Cookbook of the Jews of Greece. 1986, Cadmus Press, Port Jefferson, N.Y.
Swenson, Allan A., Plants of the Bible. Secaucus, N.J.: Carol Publishing Group, 1994
Walker, Winifred, All the Plants of the Bible. Garden City, N.Y.: Doubleday, 1957; N.Y.: Harper, 1957.
Wigoder, Deborah Emmet, The Garden of Eden Cookbook: Recipes in the Biblical Tradition. San Francisco: Harper and Row, 1988.

*See also Bibliography in Biblio Press' Miriam's Well: Rituals for Jewish Women Around the Year, by P.V. Adelman, 1986 and 1990 editions.
**This publication at P.O. Box 545, Brookline, MA 02146 contains many relevant articles on Rosh Hodesh. To learn about Rosh Hodesh groups in the USA write: The Rosh Hodesh Exchange, 20 Banks St., Somerville, MA 02144.

In times of peace,
"Judah and Israel dwelt safely, every man under
his vine and fig tree."   *I. Kings*

More Books of Good Taste From
BIBLIO PRESS

(available from your local bookstore or from Biblio Press)

MIRIAM'S WELL: *Rituals for Jewish Women Around the Year*
Second Edition 1990
By Penina V. Adelman • $11.50
Compilation of women's life cycles for use in Rosh Hodesh groups (new moon
festivals); integrates traditional and new ceremonies; the first of its kind.

FROM THE WISE WOMEN OF ISRAEL: *Folklore and Memoirs*
By Doris B. Gold and Lisa Stein • $8.95
This collection of legends, folklore and memoirs tell stories of women who perse-
vered with courage, ingenuity, wisdom and hope. These tales of wise actions and
retorts fills a gap in the genre of "wise men's tales" which usually omit women.

BURNING LIGHTS
By Bella Chagall with 36 bl/wh drawings by Marc Chagall
Intro. to 1996 ed. by Judith R. Baskin • $10.95
Reprint of 1946 memoir of Bella Chagall's life in Vitebsk, Russia pre W.W.2
"…with female experience at the center" as noted by Baskin in the Introduction.

THE VOICE OF SARAH: *Feminine Spirituality and Traditional Judaism*
By Tamar Frankiel • $9.95
This essay brings Judaism and feminism in counterpoint.
"…even orthodox women who do not question their role will find the review of
biblical passages and legends relating to women interesting…"
—Bella Hass Weinberg, D.L.S. Editor, *Judaica Librarianship*

ERNESTINE ROSE: *Women's Rights Pioneer*
By Yuri Suhl • $8.00
The only biography of this mid-19th century orator, Jewish women's rights activist,
suffragist and fragrance developer. (Perfect for Women's History Month—March)

(all above are paperbacks)

• •

Biblio Press
1140 Broadway • New York, NY 10001
TEL: (212) 684-1257 • E-MAIL: Bibook@aol.com